...and Then There Was One

Nan & Clete

...and Then There Was One

Finding a New Normal
After a Traumatic Death

Nancy S. Gibble

Nancy S. Gibble

To Pastor Chris
my story of my
"walk through the
valley of the shadow
death" —
Nan

A Not Forgotten Publication

Cover photo by Susan M. Shaw

Wedding photos by David Mosemann

Sketch on p. 73 by Nancy S. Gibble

Cover design and restoration of photos
by Larry Gainer, larryjac@earthlink.net

Internal design by Alice S. Morrow Rowan,
NotForgottenPublishing@gmail.com

Available at https://www.createspace.com/4061330
and at Amazon.com

Printed in the United States of America

Dedicated to my mother

Sara Garner Shank
1905 ~ 1954

Not a day goes by that I don't think of you

Contents

The Beginning:
A Very Good Place to Start

I just finished reading the handwritten journal I wrote in the year after Clete's accident. It made me feel, how can I possibly write about this?

I once read that, before the written word, people kept an oral history, stories passed down from generation to generation. The part I found so interesting was the fact that these oral histories were accurate. The words never changed. As I look back, I can repeat the timeline of the events of Clete's death—from the phone call I got from the police about his accident, up to his death thirty hours later—and never change a word.

My sister-in-law driving me to the hospital and dropping me off before she parked.

Waiting for the chaplain to come take me back to the ER. (That was one thing I would change; it cost me ten or fifteen precious minutes while he was still conscious.)

Seeing his horrendous facial injuries, the IVs already running.

Being told he had already had a CAT scan of his brain, that the IVs had Vitamin K and frozen plasma in them to try to stop the bleeding into his brain.

Leaning over him and telling him over and over that I loved him. All he could say was, "I don't know what happened, I don't know what happened." As they put a catheter in, he pleaded with them not to.

Hearing the trauma doctor call down to say that Mr. Gibble was deteriorating rapidly and was being sent for another CAT scan.

The next hours with the chaplain and my sister-in-law by my side as I tried to reach our four children and make sense of a world gone mad are as fresh in my memory today as if it all happened yesterday.

I want this story to be one of hope. I make no pretense that it has been an easy journey since I got that telephone call on February 20, 2006. It has been the hardest road I have ever traveled. I am a writer, and over the past six years, particularly the first four, I wrote and wrote. It was one of the things that saved my sanity.

This, then, is my story. ~

O LORD, support us all the day long, until the shadows lengthen and the evening comes, and the busy world is hushed, and the fever of life is over, and our work is done. Then in thy mercy grant us a safe lodging, and a holy rest, and peace at the last. Amen.

Book of Common Prayer, 1928

The Neurotrauma Unit

They wheeled Clete down for his second CAT scan.

The Chaplain was with me as I tried unsuccessfully to reach the children. I simply left messages and told them their Dad was in an accident and they should come to the hospital.

I then went to the neurotrauma unit, where he was sent after his test. When I walked into his room, he was lying there on his back with IVs running, in a coma.

The nurse asked me if I knew what was wrong. I replied, yes, but I did not want anything negative said in his room, because I could not be sure what he could hear. He looked so still and so uncomfortable—they still had a cervical collar on him.

I was told we would have twenty-four-hour access to him unless they were doing a procedure, and there would be a nearby room available so I could spend the night. That was a great gift.

It was probably four or five hours before three of the children arrived. My youngest son was catching a red-eye flight out of Colorado and was expected the next morning.

I briefly explained the rules. At that time I had no idea what the details of the accident were. As the evening wore on it was obvious that the prognosis was very grim.

At some point while the family was gathered together in a small room, the neurosurgeon came in to talk to us. He was very kind as he described the extent of the brain injury. He made it clear that he could not operate be-cause the damage was already so vast and would only get worse. Any surgery would do even more damage. I replied that I understood, but I was not ready to count him out. He replied, "No, and you shouldn't." I told the doctor we'd known the dangers of him riding bike because he was on an anticoagulant, but I could not ask him not to ride anymore than I could ask a bird not to fly. Dr. Gastaldo responded with support and understanding.

It was agreed that the children would go home and my youngest daughter would stay in the hospital with me as we tried to get some sleep. ~

"I am with thee, and will keep thee in all places whither thou goest."

Genesis 28:15 (KJV)

A Sleepless Night and a Small Miracle

At some point Clete was put on a ventilator and intercranial catheters were put into his brain. The blood was streaming down the side of his face. As I tried to stop it, I told Paige to call a nurse, and a doctor was called to stitch his scalp and stop the bleeding.

I would go to bed, my mind going a mile a minute. I thought of several doctor appointments he had scheduled in the next few days, one of which was to be checked to be sure he was still cancer free. Also, other people had to be notified. Paige can sleep at the drop of a hat, but she sensed when I needed her and would sit up in bed and write on a note pad what needed to be done.

I was in and out of his room and was shocked when I walked in around 2 A.M. to see his bed empty. I immediately went out to the nurses' station to ask where he was. They told me he had been taken down for another CAT scan. When I asked why, they replied it was just routine. I knew full well that nothing is "just routine" at 2:00 in the morning.

I walked out to the Starlight waiting room to just sit and think. It was so peaceful and quiet. There was a cleaning lady working. She smiled at me and I told her how nice and clean it looked and what a fine job she was doing. She smiled and we chatted a bit.

Soft music was playing in the background. As the sound washed over me and calmed me, I suddenly realized what was playing. During the year before the accident I would constantly listen to "You Lift Me Up" sung by

Sheila Walsh. It became my mantra to hold onto during a year of three surgeries for Clete and helping my sister move to an assisted living facility. It was a different artist singing it now, but what a blessing.

I felt the love of God surround me and calm me. I sat for a while and then went over to a very quiet area where I could sit and look out over James Street. It was just good to be able to feel some sort of peace in the middle of the night.

When I walked back to his room, he had returned from his latest test. I was ready to face whatever I had to. He was deteriorating rapidly. At some point I was asked if they should restart his heart if it stopped. I replied, "Absolutely not." We had talked about end-of-life issues at great length and knew we did not want our deaths prolonged if there was no hope of a quality of life. ~

The Memorial Service

I was just seventeen when I met Clete, only a few months out of high school.* We met. We dated. We fell in love. I remember thinking on our first date, "He's the nicest boy I ever met." On one date I put on (now remember, this was the fifties) the "little black dress" that I thought was the ultimate classy outfit. When Clete picked me up he took one look and said, "Are you going to a funeral?" I don't think I ever wore that dress again. So, I called my daughters together and said, nobody wears all black to the funeral. We will all wear bright colors!

We met in October 1951, he was drafted into the Army in February 1952, and we were married on the Fourth of July 1952. He had a three-day pass and we honeymooned at his army camp. He was my husband, my lover, my best friend, and the funniest person I knew. He was my hero.

Now, lest you think we had the perfect marriage, let me assure you we did not. We could fight, we had rough times—in short, we were like everybody else. But even when we didn't *like* each other, we always *loved* each other. I knew I could trust him with my life, and he could trust me with his.

Fifty-three years ago we stood before God and promised to be faithful, to love and to hold each other—and we

---

* I gave this eulogy at Clete's funeral at St. Paul's United Church of Christ, Manheim, Pennsylvania.

honored those promises. As we grew older, we both became absolutely convinced that should something happen and we would have no quality of life, we did not want our death prolonged. We made a promise we would not let that happen. We asked our children to support us in that.

Biking was his passion, his therapy, his love. As most of you know, it had been a stressful year for us, Clete had a medicated stent put in last March, and complications: he developed a hernia that could not be operated on for six months, and finally, right before he had that surgery, he was diagnosed with bladder cancer. Through it all he kept working and, with his doctor's blessing, kept riding his bike.

Just a few weeks ago, as he was finally regaining his strength and feeling really well again, he went out for a ride. I was sitting in the living room reading when he came home. I looked up and he was standing there, his face pink from the cold air and the greatest grin on his face. I said, "You had a great ride, didn't you?"

"Oh yes, I really did."

I thought, "I wish I had a camera." He looked like he had hung the moon.

I thought he was amazing, this seventy-five-year-old guy who could still do the MS charity ride every year and ride 150 miles in one weekend. He loved that weekend and raising money for that charity.

Then, on Monday he went out for what was to be his last ride. When the police called me, the details were sketchy. The officer just asked me to please not drive to the hospital by myself. I called his sister in what turned out to be one of the best decisions of my life.

I do not believe that this tragedy was God's will—but God did allow it to happen. I do know that from the point of the accident to the time of his death, God was with us every step of the way. I got to the hospital to be met by a chaplain. He took me back to Clete and I could see that this was not good, but he knew me. I leaned down and kissed his poor battered face and kissed him and kissed him and told him I loved him over and over. He looked at me out of the only eye he could open—I can't describe his expression—he just kept saying, "I don't know what happened." I kept trying to comfort him and told him I loved him, while his kid sister was on his other side. God was in that emergency room. He was there in the chaplain, in the trauma doctor; he was there when he gave me the gift of being able to say goodbye to my husband, because had I gotten there fifteen or twenty minutes later, any verbal communication would have been over.

My children tell me I was strong. They are wrong; I was determined—and they helped me to be strong. I was determined that this man was going to be fiercely protected. The very first rule was that no one was allowed to say anything negative in his room. Everyone honored that wish—from family to staff. He was cared for in the most loving, professional manner, by the best nurses and doctors. By Monday evening, things looked very grim, but I continued to hope for a miracle. By Tuesday morning, when I talked to the most kind and compassionate doctor, I knew that miracle was not going to happen. He was already on a ventilator as I stroked his face and told him that for fifty-three years we had kept our promises and I was now going to keep this last promise to him, the hardest one I had to keep.

God was with me when I made the decision to have him taken off the ventilator. I asked the children to leave. The nurse said I might want to leave while they removed the tubing. I declined; no way was he making any part of this journey alone.

In the hours that followed we did sing him home. I heard Paige tell her Dad, "You're almost there, Dad. You're almost there," and then, "Oh Dad, you're home now," in a joyous voice.

I kept my promise to the man who had cared for me so lovingly all these years. With his passing he took a part of me, the best part, with him. Never a day will pass that I won't want him and our life back the way it was just a short thirty hours before.

The words to a few verses of the following song speak volumes as to how my hero made me feel:

I do not have a fortune to buy
you pretty things
but I can weave you moonbeams
for necklaces and rings.

I can show you morning
on a thousand hills
and kiss you and give you
seven daffodils.*

Thanks, Clete, for a life well lived. ~

---

* "Seven Daffodils" by Lee Hayes and Fran Moseley, 1957.

Early Days and a New Land

I was surrounded and protected by my family that first week. They fielded all the telephone calls, made sure I ate, helped plan the memorial service. The second week, my youngest son delayed flying home to Colorado to stay with me.

As I look over my journal from that time, I see that I wrote, it is like living in a strange country, a new land, and you are pretty sure you are never going to like it and now it is too hard to find a new best friend that you've left behind and you are absolutely sure you will never find another one like the one you've lost. The question becomes, will your life ever be bearable with that gigantic hole in your heart?

One does tend to think in run-on sentences, as though your mind is hotwired.

In those first weeks I thought I was literally losing my mind. I clearly remember pouring a bowl of cereal and the box was empty. I stood there holding it, in a panic, thinking, now what do I do? I have no cereal! I started to put on a pot of coffee and could not remember how. I became very frightened and walked into my living room, where there was some literature on sudden death and the grieving process. One of the statements was, "You will feel like you are losing your mind."

A very healing part in the beginning was thinking how awed I was at the number of people who came to his memorial service—so many that people had to be turned away. Ah, and the cards and letters: 450 in all and every one a treasure. I took to waiting till bedtime to read them. I would crawl into bed and go through the fifty or more cards that had come that day. Sure it made me cry, but those were good tears.

I was fortunate that every time I went out, people would stop and talk to me and reminisce about Clete. One day at the local supermarket I ran into a friend. She was going on and on about what a great guy Clete was, how he always smiled and had a good word. We were talking and laughing and finally I said, "Gee, if I would have known he was such a great guy I might have been a better wife!" She looked shocked at first and then we both burst out laughing.

You need that kind of humor and Clete had it in spades.

The night of his death, my daughters and youngest son stayed because I said I couldn't leave until Ted, our friend and funeral director, came for his body. The nurse told me it might be a long time because it was a coroner's case. I was very upset at the idea of an autopsy. She explained it was the law because a car was involved, but since the cause of death was obvious, she doubted they would do one.

I was exhausted and apologized to the children— it was just something I needed to do. Then I looked at Clete and said of course I knew he'd say, "What are you doing sitting around with a dead guy?" Their eyes got wide as they looked at me, and then we all laughed because that is exactly what he would have said.

My son finally persuaded me to let his sister take me home and he and my other daughter would wait. Up to that point the only tears I had shed were when I stood by his bed and said I was going to keep one last promise to him, the hardest one I ever had to keep.

I went home, got into bed, and then the tears started and I couldn't stop. My son told me later, as he was in the next room he thought, "That is the saddest sound I have ever heard." For the next year I cried. ~

"Grieving is as natural as crying when you are hurt, sleeping when you are tired, eating when you are hungry, or sneezing when your nose itches. It is nature's way of healing a broken heart."

Doug Manning,
Don't Take My Grief Away

The Last Birthday Card

God can take your breath away.

The past is where we met
fell in love, married
I LOVE OUR PAST

The present is where
we live as partners
and best friends . . .
I LOVE OUR PRESENT

and I love you —
Happy 75—in years
much younger in spirit
your biggest fan, Nan

and the future —
well, I LOVE OUR FUTURE
because we'll be in it together

Happy Birthday,
My husband, my love

I found this card, the last birthday card I had sent to him, and I had signed it after the second part. I didn't notice the last part of the card until three months after he died, as I was making his memory book. I cried. I hadn't known our future would be only ten short months.

I also found in his prayer journal for that year, "Thank you, Lord, for letting me live to be 75." ~

"If you were going to die soon and had only one phone call you could make, who would you call and what would you say? And why are you waiting?"

Stephen Levine, *A Year to Live*

The Broken Jar

Six or seven years ago, when my husband and I were vacationing in Cape May, New Jersey, I bought a little blue-and-white jar and soap dish set. The jar was so pretty in shades of blues with a sliver of a moon on the outer rim of the lid, and white rabbits gamboling among the grasses in the moonlight.*

I put it in our powder room and became very attached to the little blue jar. It just made me smile to look at it.

One day my husband came walking out of the powder room holding the broken pieces of the jar in his hands. He had dropped it; a piece had broken out of the bottom and a larger piece out of the lid, just beside the sliver of moon. The odd thing was, we could not find the missing pieces to try to mend it. I knew he thought I would be upset, but I just said, "Oh well, I'll try to find another sometime," and put it back in the powder room.

From time to time, if I thought of it, I would look for something to replace it. When we got back to Cape May I went to the store where I had bought it, hoping they would still carry them. Of course they did not.

Time went on and I kind of forgot about it. Clete was having some health problems and it had been a stressful several months. I looked at that little jar one day, picked

---

* Originally published in the *Lancaster Sunday News*.

it up, and walked out to where my husband was reading the morning paper. As he looked up at me I said, "You know what? I'm not going to replace this little jar, because I decided if I were broken, you wouldn't get rid of me." He just kind of smiled and didn't say anything.

Several months later he died from the injuries he suffered in the bicycling accident.

I forgot about the jar until, one day several months after his death, I dropped it. The lid completely broke in half this time. I thought, oh no, quickly picked it up and, knowing it was a lost cause, went to search for some glue.

Miracles are in the small things.

The glue held. The little jar still sits in my powder room. Whenever I look at it, I smile and feel good. It has become a symbol to me of the love my husband and I shared and how even in the hard times there is a glue that keeps love strong and steadfast. ~

How Do I Feel?

Today it is six months since my love died. My therapist asks me how that feels. Sometimes I stumble through the answer at session, but most of the time I think the answer through over a period of days or even weeks.

Thinking about that question as I drove up to the cemetery to place flowers on Clete's grave, it seems in some ways that it happened only yesterday. It is all still so fresh in my mind. The telephone ringing, the officer telling me I should get to the hospital. The thirty hours until his death seem as close and as real as they did that day.

In other ways I cannot believe I have survived for six months. The hurt and the grief have been so much harder. Maybe *harder* is not the right word. In the beginning one is in shock and for a good month or two you go on autopilot, doing what must be done and trying to make sense of a life turned upside down.

After I fixed the flowers on his grave I stepped back to see how pretty they looked. I leaned up against another tombstone and started talking to him. Since the picture is up, I feel much closer to him. I cried a bit, but they were good tears as I recalled our life together; then there were the not so good tears of regret for a life so cruelly taken. I turned and looked up at the sky. It was a beautiful day and there were many clouds, which are always comforting to me. I kept scanning the sky and cloud after cloud looked like dolphins, porpoises, whales, and sea lions. I had to grin and think of how much we loved the ocean, how much we loved spotting the sea creatures.

My visits to the cemetery have become a healing place for me. I am anxious for the stone with the verses of "Seven Daffodils" to go up. Some probably think I am insane to go to all this trouble, but I know better. It was a kind of insanity, but I make no apologies for that. Widowhood brings a kind of freedom to be as weird as you want to be.

Some days my life feels so empty that it is a deep pain I think will never go away, a loneliness so intense it will literally destroy me. Somehow I go on and occasionally have a day where I feel almost "normal."

I would gladly give my life to have his back again. I think I cry for all the years gone by and want to live it all again—only this time be smarter, nicer, better, perfect. Ah, and wouldn't that be a boring life.

~ October 21, 2006 ~

The tombstone with the three verses from the Seven Daffodils song was put up last week. I waited for a sunny day to go see it.

How lovely it is! I was so excited and happy. I threw my hands in the air, twirled around, and shouted to the sky, "I did it honey. I did it, and all by myself!" I felt glorious. Clete would probably shake his head and think I'm insane to care so much, but it was important to me. He loves me and he would understand. How I love that guy. ~

Weep with Those Who Weep

Andrew was a toddler when I first knew him. I felt a special affection for this little guy.*

He was ten when my husband died from his injuries in a bicycling accident. Andrew's family was very good to me, including me in their large family gatherings. I could always count on a hug from Andrew whenever I saw him. That was a great gift for a lady with a broken heart.

Nine months after my husband died the church held its annual service in remembrance of those who had died the previous year. It is always a very emotional service. As the pastor reads the name of each one who died, the church bells toll and a candle is lit in their honor.

I felt someone quietly slip into the pew beside me. I looked and said, "Oh, Andrew." He looked at me with eyes so full of concern. I took his hand. As the service went on I was in tears and he put his arm around my shoulder, gently comforting me. At the conclusion of the service, family members are invited to come forward and receive a candle and a flower. I looked at Andrew and asked if he would go forward with me. I rejoiced that God was at work in this child.

We left the service and he walked me to the exit. I hugged him and thanked him for being there with me. It was a bitterly cold November day. He looked at me and said,

---

* Title from Romans 12:15, *Today's English Version*. Originally published in the newsletter of St. Paul's United Church of Christ, Manheim.

"Stay warm." My heart *was* warm, and comforted, because one of God's children had a heart as big as the world.

Andrew is fourteen now and this year I was privileged to be his mentor in our church. Sometimes I think that is backward. He has been an example to me of the power of reaching out to a hurting heart.

Dear Lord, thank you for the children, for in them we truly see the glory of God. ~

"Lord, teach us how to be present with those who need comfort, when to comfort with silence and when to comfort with words."

Paula Geister

Life Is Complicated

Looking back, I realize I was in shock for a far longer period than I realized at the time. I know that made it hard for my family. I also know I was not what they wanted me to be. I was not what I wanted me to be!

Early on, Alta said this is not about family history, this is about Clete being dead and no one knows how to live without him. I'm still trying to learn that and feel I haven't gotten very far. Every day is hard—from simply wanting to turn the clock back to February 19th to learning how to do everything without him.

He was very proud of his children, these bright, beautiful, and handsome daughters and sons. He loved and adored Ben. I grieve not just for what I lost, but for what he will never see—his grandson's graduation and marriage and oh so many more things.

They all thought I was strong—I knew that I was not. This is a woman who only last week could not figure out if she was on the right road to the therapist, who walks around with a light bulb in her purse so she doesn't forget to buy one. Who never asks anyone over for a meal because some days she can barely figure out what to feed herself. I take a step forward and then feel like I am taking two or ten steps back. It is just the way it is—I live in hope that someday it will be better.

I too am proud of our children and hope that someday things will be better. I would love to sit and talk about their memories of their dad. To go through old journals kept by their paternal grandfather and by their dad.

It has been only nine months since he died; that is such a tiny time when you consider I knew him for more than fifty-four years. ~

"People ask me if I'm healing. Healing? Why should I heal? What's wrong with rupture? Living with Rupture—sounds like the title of a best seller to me. I've been reading books lately about losing spouses, by Joan Didion, Nora Ephron, Donald Hall, plus a few how-to's on widowhood, and I'm getting a little fed up with everyone's trying to avoid self-pity. If not now, for goodness sake, then when? Actually, I've become a welcome wagon for both Self-Pity and her more important brother, Grief. The three of us are thicker than thieves."

Sally Ryder Brady, *A Box of Darkness*

Grief Wears Two Different Pairs of Shoes

Today it is nine months ago that my husband of fifty-three years died from his injuries sustained in a bicycling accident. With his death, my world as I had known it ended.*

As I reflect on all my different feelings as I travel this long and lonely road, I think back to last week. I had a doctor appointment and, as women will do, put on two different pairs of shoes to decide which I liked best with my outfit. I know you are ahead of me here. As I stepped out of my car, I looked down and thought, "Oh, my word, I have on two different pairs of shoes." I kind of made everyone's day in Mt. Joy.

I was telling the therapist, whom I have been seeing since Clete's death, that story. We both were laughing and then she said, "Nan, grief is wearing two different pairs of shoes. You must write a story about that." Wow—what a wonderful analogy. That's why she's the therapist and I'm the patient.

In the beginning you can drive yourself crazy with the "what ifs" and "if onlys." One shoe is trying to change what is while the other shoe is trying to find comfort. My comfort at first came in unexpected ways before I could even think. While waiting in the hospital in the middle of the night for them to bring Clete back from

---

* Originally published in the *Lancaster Sunday News* "I Know a Story" column.

his third CAT scan, I heard a praise song I had come to love in the months before the accident. I heard it again at an Italian bakery in downtown Lancaster, sung in Italian no less. I heard it again, a month or two later, after a very bad day, in the middle of Savemart. Some may call that coincidence. I prefer to call it the hand of God.

Looking back, I realize I was in shock for much longer then I thought at the time. I instinctively turned to our wedding pictures. I loved looking at them—we were so young. He taught me so much. Neither of us knew who we really were or what we would become. We learned together and were always the most important person in each other's life.

I decided to make a memory book of photos to celebrate our life together. That was marvelously healing. It put our life in perspective. It helped me to see that being beset by regrets after a sudden death is very natural. That our life together was one giant mosaic made up of many pieces and every part was important. That shoe was pointing me to something that helped me heal even as I cried.

That other shoe has and still does pull me back as I deal with the multiple unpleasant tasks of being a widow. I had a very hard time the first time I had to check that word on a form. Grief is a roller coaster and it lasts much, much longer then one can ever dream. The holidays are particularly hard—he is not here. My instinct is to crawl into bed, pull the covers over my head, and not emerge until January 15th, at the earliest! Because my mother died when I was twenty, the holidays have always been bittersweet for me. It is always hard to see mothers and daughters doing things together.

Early June, when he would have retired from his second full-time job, was particularly hard. As I searched for something to help me through the downward spiral, I decided to make patchwork pillows out of his shirts and give them to family members to comfort them as Father's Day approached. That has been a shoe that has brought me great joy. It has become therapy for me. I made many for family, extended family, and myself. They are the best things in the world to cry into, to just have one in your lap or bed. I soon started giving them to friends who were going through hard times. I call them "Clete's comfort pillows." Sometimes I give them as thank-you pillows to people who have been there for me at an especially hard time.

Yes, grief is wearing two different pair of shoes. The shoe that lets you take tiny steps toward learning to live without the brightest star in your life. The shoe that just stays beside you as you cry endless tears—so many that you feel you should have an IV running to replace the lost fluids. The shoe that throws what seems like the last straw as you realize you must deal with yet another insurance problem and you just know you can't do one more thing. But then there is always the shoe that helps you pick yourself up and get through one more day.

I often joked over the years that no one knew my real name. I was always Clete Gibble's wife, or Alan, Bethany, Paige, or Matt's mother. Indeed, among the hundreds of cards I got after his death was one from a friend who said she always thought Clete-and-Nan was one word.

There is one picture in my memory book that I love. Clete is leaning against a lamp post in Puerto Rico, where we had gone on a mission trip. He looks so handsome. I wrote in the book beside that photo:

"He took this little girl and showed her the moon, the places I never dreamed I'd go—he taught me to love, he taught me trust. He kept me safe, but most of all he made my life a glorious adventure."

This shoe gives me hope, and I realize how proud I am to be known as Clete Gibble's wife. Thank you, darling. ~

"Hope" is the thing with feathers —
That perches in the soul —
And sings the tune without the words —
And never stops — at all —

Emily Dickinson

Take Two Doses of Reality and Call Me in the Morning

Clete was an avid supporter of the MS Charity Bike ride and participated for many years. He had already signed up for the ride before his death. Five of us from the family decided to do the ride in his honor the July after his death.

He would do 100 miles on Saturday and 50 to 75 miles on Sunday. We each did 25 miles. He had raised a great deal of money over the years. We all set to raising money, something I do not like to do.

Clete and I always worked as a team. I was his biggest cheerleader when he did the ride. Our summers revolved around his training and the actual weekend ride. We planned our vacations around that. I was his secretary, sending out letters to possible contributors. He asked people he worked with and our church family to support him.

I was amazed when I was able to raise $3,100 so soon after his death, because many people had contributed to that charity when he died. I mentioned to a family member that I was the tenth highest fundraiser. They remarked, that was because of Dad. That statement bothered me, but it took me a day or two to figure out why.

I thought back to a friend I had run into a day or so before that conversation. She was complimenting me on my article in the newspaper, and as we talked I mentioned how kind and caring people had been to me. Then I said, but of course that is all because of Clete. She became very angry and said, "Oh no, don't sell yourself short. This is because people love and admire you." I repeated that story to Alta at my next session. Her eyes flashed and she said, "Good for her. She is exactly right. I cannot believe all the things you have done to heal yourself."

My friend did me a great favor by telling me not to sell myself short. Alta tells me I should write a book. Perhaps someday I will. She also suggested I make a list of all I have had to deal with since his death. I did that and listed ninety-eight different things. I told Alta no one would want to read the book I would write, it would just be too depressing!

January 1st was by far worse than Christmas because he was never alive in 2007. The thought of February 20th and 21st fills me with a feeling of utter panic. I will probably go away for a few days. Going away by myself gives me some of my most peaceful times.

I have been humbled and awed by the reaction to the article I had in the *Sunday News*. That article has been copied by many people and shared with others who are grieving. To have Hospice handing it out at their early bereavement sessions is very gratifying.

I had sent the article to Don Green, our friend from Clete's basic training days when he was in the Army. He wrote back, "About a hundred years ago, I used to try to teach high school kids to write. I wish I could claim you as one of my students. You really do have a very natural style that has both flair and clarity." He then went on to comment on the discussions going on for years about which is harder on the surviving spouse, the quick and totally unexpected death or what Nancy Reagan called the "long goodbye." Don has been saying the long good-bye for eight years to Lois and has never deserted her. I think that however one has to face a terrible loss is the worst it could possibly be. There is no right or wrong way to grieve. It is not a contest.

Thanks to one of Clete's cardiologists who steered me in the right direction, I got the courage to get Clete's records and his CAT scans from the hospital. The records ran to 126 pages. It took me three hours to go over them and flag the different injuries and procedures I had questions about. Dr. Peter Stewart, the trauma doctor who was in charge of Clete's case from the ER to his death, graciously took the time to sit and go over everything with me. He is a wonderful, kind, and caring man. I also have an appointment to talk to Dr. Gohn, one of Clete's cardiologists. To me, knowledge is power and gives me some kind of closure—no matter how hard it is to relive those terrible thirty hours. I was completely undone the day after I spoke to Dr. Stewart, but I am glad I did.

I have gotten past the "St. Clete" scenario. I finally realized that I was making him Mr. Perfect and me a real merde. One morning I woke up and said, oh honey, I was such a jerk sometimes. I then started laughing and said, but so were you.

What really broke me of the "St. Clete" idea happened on my birthday. I was sitting at the kitchen table crying and crying because he wasn't with me on my birthday. I thought, we met when I was seventeen and this is the first birthday he is not with me. Suddenly I stopped crying and thought, now wait a minute—he was a hunter, he was never even *home* on my birthday for probably forty some years.

Yeah, a few doses of reality are good for your mental health. ~

A Miracle in Two Parts

Two are better off than one, because to-gether they can work more effectively. If one of them falls down, the other can help him up. But if someone is alone and falls, it's just too bad, because there is no one to help him. If it is cold, two can sleep together and stay warm, but how can you keep warm by yourself?

Ecclesiastes 4:9–11 GNT

I woke feeling uneasy and sad. I lay there with all kinds of random thoughts going through my mind and feeling so clearly the need to feel loved and protected.

Then, as clear as if Clete were still alive, I felt him touch my shoulder. He leaned down and kissed me on the nape of my neck and said in his lover's gentle voice, "Well, maybe we can take care of that tonight."

It was the first time since his death that I actually felt his presence and heard his voice just as he spoke in life. What a gift. It was so real and special and I felt so loved. Thank you, God.

I was still in bed, just thinking about this miracle, when the telephone rang. It was my friend Marti Harnish. She had been much on my mind the last week or so. I knew I wanted to touch base with her about going to Savannah. As we talked and she told me how much she had been thinking of me and praying for me last week, I shared some of the things I had been going through and then shared the experience I'd just had. We cried together.

We then went on to discuss the Savannah trip and decided we both wanted to do that. She is having her daughter research airfare and B&B accommodations.

That was miracle number two, because I am so ready for a trip and although I could have gone alone, it is so special that a friend wants to make the trip with me. I am excited. ~

One Toothbrush
and Matching Towels

Alta asked me at my last session, what were some of the things that were really hard and what were some that were not as hard as I had expected?

As always, I can come up with answers quickly, but then I think about the question more in depth the next week.

Two things bothered me terribly right away, as I was cleaning the bathroom. First, I threw his toothbrush in the waste can. But then, as I looked at that toothbrush holder, I simply could not stand the sight of it with only one lonely toothbrush. I pulled his out of the can and to this day I still have his toothbrush in one of my bathrooms. The other thing that bothered me was hanging up clean towels. We always had matching towels and I could not stand the sight of one towel hanging there. I went out and bought all new towels—one of each in completely different colors. All our other towels I gave away.

Why would those two things bother me so much? I have no idea, but at least they were easy things to fix.

One thing I thought would bother me terribly turned out to be not so bad: going to bed without the man I had slept beside for almost fifty-four years. However, getting awake in the morning and not having him beside me is heartbreaking.

The last two days as I think about the one-year anniversary of the terrible phone call to go to the hospital and the next thirty hours until his death, I have been crying almost constantly—deep, heart-rending sobs—and my heart breaks all over again.

What has been far better than I expected is the support I have gotten from our sons. They have been magnificent. In fact, the only time I felt true happiness in this past year was when Matt came home to help and we went to the Horse Inn for dinner with Alan and Marti. We had such a good time talking and reminiscing and laughing. As I lay in bed that night I thought, "Oh my, I actually feel happy. What a wonderful feeling, I forgot what that was like." I have not felt that since, but it lets me know that happiness is out there somewhere and I will feel it again.

It was much more difficult between my daughters and me. I was simply not much good at doing more than caring for myself. They were always very close to their father, so it was very difficult for them also. From all my readings, I get this is not that unusual. Still, it was very painful for us.

What has been extremely stressful is learning all the ins and outs of our finances, insurance, doing every little thing that needs to be taken care of. Alan is wonderful about taking care of the car and any chores I can't manage. Dealing with social security has been hard. There too I had help from a dear friend from church.

It makes me feel good (and at times proud), all I have been able to accomplish. Not having someone to vent my frustrations to, even if he is listening with only half an ear, is hard. He was my safe place, always, and that is gone forever.

I am grateful that we moved to the townhouse. He loved it and so do I. I am surrounded by many happy memories. It also has become my safe haven.

One of the hardest things is having to be in control of everything, having to make every decision and hoping it is the right one, not having him to bounce things off of. He did me a great favor in being so well organized and made everything easier, but I do not like having to make all decisions by myself.

Weekends can be OK or very bad. Sometimes I look forward to the quiet of them, if I've had a very busy week. Sometimes they seem just endless and terribly lonely.

I found that thinking about the holidays was worse than the actual day. Once I realized I must not try to live up to other people's expectations of what I should do but just do what is right for me, it was much better.

I was not prepared for the devastation I have been feeling coming up to the one-year mark. For me it is two-part: the phone call and the death. I think this is almost worse than the actual experience, because I certainly was in a state of shock for a long time. At the hospital, I felt in control, because I was so focused on seeing he was well cared for and would have an easy going into that dark night. But now I look back on it and know the outcome and how nothing I could have done would have changed it. The raw, awful pain of his death is in some ways even worse—the feeling that I wish I had not left him alone for an instant. I know this is irrational.

Part of that feeling may be because I had just finished reading the twenty-five love letters he wrote to me before and in the early part of our marriage. Over and over again he tells me how much he misses me and wants me near him, that life without me would be meaningless. It made me realize how important I was in his life when he was going through hard times. So I suppose I feel I should have been superhuman and never left his side.

On the other hand, I am thankful that we lived in a time when people actually wrote letters by hand. Imagine the gift of having twenty-five letters from the love of your life. Priceless!

One thing that has happened since he died that simply amazes me is the outpouring of love and support I have gotten from coworkers, friends, church family, perfect strangers—the fact that even after all this time there are many who have been steadfast in their support and caring.

I have also been grateful that through my writings and my pillow project I have been able to reach out to people while at the same time helping myself. My writing is very therapeutic even when I just write at random and am not writing for publication. It is interesting to look back months later and see what I was thinking at that time.

Strangely, some things that I thought would be hard were not in the beginning and now are becoming more so. One of those is eating alone, probably because my eating habits early on were very erratic. Now, some days I can sit down at the breakfast table and burst into tears with loneliness. I have found that eating in the dining room when those feelings are very bad is a help. We seldom used the dining room in this house except for company or in the summer when we were grilling. It seems I do a tap dance around certain things until I figure out how to lessen the pain.

Of course sometimes there is no way around anything and I just cry and cry until I am exhausted. I have found that "getting out of Dodge" for a few days where nobody knows your name is very healing.

I think I am making progress in the fact that I realize I can do pretty much anything I need to in the practical line—but not so much progress in dealing with the terrible pain and loss I feel about the accident and subsequent death.

My writing seems to be the best therapy of all—except for Alta, of course.

When I took a Quest class on religion some years ago, one of the speakers, a Catholic priest, said that praying for healing and the body does not get healed does not mean prayer was not answered, because the soul can be healed even if the body isn't.

I love that. Even though I do not remember praying for Clete's healing, because I knew almost instantly how severe his injuries were, I still find that very comforting. ~

"May God grant you always
A sunbeam to warm you
A moonbeam to charm you
A sheltering Angel
So nothing can harm you
Laughter to cheer you
Faithful friends near you—
And whenever you pray
Heaven to hear you."

Irish Blessing

Who? Me?

Sometimes Alta asks hard questions. This week at session she asked me two. The first was what I would tell people about how I got from the beginning to this point a bit more than a year later.

After much thought, the first thing I would say is that I do not want to be a role model for anyone. Everyone's grief is different. I do know that it is the hardest job I have ever had.

One of the most important things, I would say, is to follow your own instincts and do whatever feels right for you. I was fortunate enough to know instantly that I would need to see a counselor, and blessed to have a caring person guide me to a very gifted one. One who is exactly right for me. I also knew I needed safe places and anything that did not feel safe I avoided.

Do not be surprised if your help comes from the most unexpected places. The flip side is that the support you would have thought you could depend on may not be there. In the land of traumatic deaths, that is not unique. Making peace with it is essential to your own healing.

Since I have always had a hard time asking for help, I was fortunate to have people in my life who reached out to me. In the beginning I could barely take telephone calls.

But there are many things one has to do whether one wants to or not. Dealing with lawyers, insurance carriers, financial advisors, tax accounts, social security, Medicare, lock boxes, and trips to the courthouse was like being in a foreign land.

It did give me a certain feeling of strength that during the worst time of my life I learned to navigate those roads. Sometimes I made mistakes and though one of those mistakes turned out to be quite costly, it was not the end of the world. I had to learn not to beat myself up if I stumbled. I did the best I could.

I was extremely lucky to have been married to a man who respected my abilities. Therefore I was not as much in the dark as some women, or men for that matter, would have been in the same circumstances. He did me a great favor in being meticulous in keeping good records. It helped me immeasurably. I thought often, well, how would Clete do this? I did come to realize eventually that I did not have to do everything the way we would have if he had lived to take his retirement. After all, things had changed and it was OK if I did not do everything the same way.

I would advise anyone, if asked, to try to find something that helps you through the deep pain. For me, from the very beginning it was looking at our wedding pictures. That segued into going through all our old photos and making a memory book of the photos, cards to each other, and memories of our life together. That was amazingly healing to me. I still pull that out from time to time. In the beginning, every time I looked at it I cried. Now, mostly I smile and laugh.

The other thing that helped me more than I can say is deciding to make what I call "Clete's comfort pillows" out of his clothing. At last count I think I've made seventy pillows. I have given them to many people, either in thanks for being kind to me or because they are going through their own hard times. At one point I was having a particularly hard time of it. I thought, I must get out the sewing machine and make pillows. It was extremely therapeutic. My need to do that is no longer strong. It seems my need and the clothing available to do it ran out at almost the same time. God has a way of blessing us in ways we would never imagine.

My greatest help from the clergy came from the hospital chaplain who was on call when Clete died. He helped me tremendously, kept in touch with me after Clete died, sent me articles, and had lunch with me one day at my request.

I have a very strong faith and was grateful that I was never angry with God or with Clete for riding bike. That is not to say I did not have some painful conversations with God. The great thing about God is that—even when I was brokenhearted with grief and sometimes just unable to find comfort—God never gives up on us. I have known that for a long time. It gave me no comfort at all to think Clete was in a "better place." I simply wanted him back and I wanted our life back. I still do. I suspect I always will.

What would I tell people? A friend wrote and told me that after his wife's death someone said to him, "It gets worse and then it gets better and then it gets worse." I have found those words to be exactly right on. Life is definitely a roller coaster. My worst time came six months after Clete's death and lasted a full eight weeks. In some ways I am doing better. While I hate handling all the finances, I can do it. The one-year anniversary was far harder than I anticipated it would be. One just seems to have to go through those dark periods of the soul.

If I'm having an especially hard time, I need alone time. I think of it as a dog licking his wounds and crawling into a cave to heal. It took me almost a year to be able to make plans to go to Colorado to see Matt and his family, a little more time than that to be able to plan a trip with a friend to Savannah. I am actually looking forward to those trips. That is a huge step forward for me. I have to cry to think of not being able to share those times with him, but they are not tears of deep despair as my earlier tears were.

Another thing that was, and continues to be, very healing is going away for two or three days by myself. Checking into a hotel or a B&B and doing only what I feel like doing is balm for my soul. I think I will continue to do that. It is good to go where "nobody knows your name."

My job and staying on the search committee for a new pastor at church have been life savers for me. They are places where I have good friends, where I have to do a job and do it well. It gives me something worthwhile to think about, places where I can laugh and feel like I am worth something.

One of the most important things is my writing. For many years I have kept a prayer journal and found it very rewarding. After Clete died, to look back at my journal and at one he kept was at times painful, but also very gratifying. It is precious to have things in his handwriting. I have also found as I look back over what I have written since his death that, had I not recorded those thoughts and happenings, I would not have remembered certain events. My writings help me see more clearly where I am and what I feel. My one article on grief, published since his death, has given me a great feeling of being able to reach out to other people who are hurting. I was awed and humbled by the response to that article and it has had a ripple effect on those whose lives it has touched.

Deciding to get a copy of the records and CAT scans from his time in the hospital was a good choice. I was lucky enough to have Clete cared for by a very kind and compassionate doctor. Many cared for him over those thirty hours, but Dr. Peter Stewart was in charge of his case. While going over those records and looking at the films was very painful, it was also enormously helpful. It answered some unanswered questions and put everything in a time frame for me.

As I write this, I still try to think of an answer to the question, "What would you tell people about how you got from there to here?" The idea that I have anything special to share does make me feel like *Who? Me?*

I stumble, I fall, and I pick myself up again. I mourn over and over for all I have lost, and yet I rejoice in having had such a great life and having shared it with such a special person. I miss everything about having him here. I really don't know what I would tell people. There is no magic way. I know I am better in some ways. I also know that I still get enormously tired and still feel very sad. One does get tired of feeling sad much of the time. This is not to say that I don't laugh and joke and have fun. Still, nothing is the same without him. I think I am forever changed, and I don't know who I will become.

One of my strengths is that I am not afraid of death and have not been for a very long time. No, it is not death one fears, but the manner of one's dying. What frightens me is that I may not have the same kind of advocate to ease my going as I was to Clete. I trusted him to be able to follow my wishes—we trusted each other with our lives, and with our deaths.

I know that life does go on and I am trying to find my place in a life without him. I know that I do not ever want to get to the place where I forget him or can't remember the sound of his voice. That to me would be the cruelest blow of all.

What would I say? Trust your instincts, take care of yourself. If you need help, ask. That is a very hard one and I was not good at that. Don't make any rash decisions. The decisions you had to make early—have someone sit down with you and re-visit them in three or four months. That can be crucial. Don't be hard on yourself. Regrets and trying to please other people take far too much energy. There is no right or wrong way to handle a loved one's death. See a counselor if you want to. That saved my life. I have no new or earth-shattering advice. Many people have to deal with a traumatic death—but going through it is more painful than I ever dreamed.

I am just an ordinary woman trying to find her way and live a life that would make Clete proud and give me peace. ~

The Second Easter

Today is the second Easter since my darling died—the first one that I could bring myself to go to church. I went downtown to First Presbyterian in Lancaster. I thought that would be easier.

Where is the justice? I thought. I lost the most important person in my life and here I sit alone and heartbroken. When will this be better?

As Pastor Riggs began his sermon I wondered if I would find any comfort. I was already in my "flight" mode; I just wanted to be home. Even as he talked about the eternal life beyond this one, I could not quite connect. I just wanted Clete back so desperately.

Then he told the story of his mother's death last November 6th. He said she was eighty-seven and ready to die. A fellow pastor ministered to her so that Pastor Riggs could be her son and not her pastor at that time. The pastor told the story of seeing her the day before her death. He called her name and she did not answer. It reminded the pastor of the story of Enoch and his walk with God. Supposedly Enoch did not die but simply passed into eternity walking with God. As God held his hand, He said to Enoch, "We have come so far and it is better for you to come with me to eternity than to go back." The pastor said to Pastor Riggs, "I thought perhaps that is what your mother did; she walked with God and had gone too far to turn back."

It brought me to tears as I thought, is that what happened to Clete? After he lapsed into his coma had he gone too far? When I decided to take him off the ventilator and crawled into bed with him, was he on that long walk with God to that beautiful place? Was it as peaceful for him as that? I pray that is true.

I have come far on this terrible journey. I have so far to go. I do not see anywhere ahead of me the peace I seek, the acceptance that I will have to learn.

To think that God did reach out his hand for Clete to grasp and hold on to is a comfort I did not think of before. I know he is whole and healthy—why then am I still so brokenhearted and desolate? ~

Be Careful What You Wish For

It wasn't a Martin Luther King sort of dream. Quite the opposite.

For weeks I had been feeling uneasy, sad, wondering whether I would ever be "OK." In fact, I had taken to answering people who asked me how I was, "OK," with a smile. Of course, I was far from OK.

I seemed so out of touch with Clete. I struggled with the feeling that his soul was not at rest and I longed for a dream.

Last night I had a dream. We were outdoors on a vacation in a foreign land, watching a show I can only describe as very opulent and risqué. The actors and actresses were very scantily clad. We were laughing and suddenly one of the actors came over and picked Clete up, put him over his shoulders, and started up an outdoor stairway as the cast kept singing and dancing.

I remember I had my hands to my face when suddenly the dancer threw Clete off his shoulders and he landed very hard on the concrete pavement. A woman beside me said, "Oh, why did he do that? I hope he's not hurt." I ran over to him and asked if he was all right.

He looked at me and sort of smiled, and then suddenly he had this perplexed look on his face and said, "No, I think something is wrong with my shoulder." I asked what he'd said to the dancer. Clete replied, "I only said, not that I'm making any moral judgment or anything, but are you—and with that he threw me off his shoulder."

"Why on earth did you say something like that?"

Then I woke up. My first thought was, why would I act as though it was Clete's fault that some nut would throw him off his shoulders, when he was the innocent victim.

As I lay there thinking about the dream, I wondered if this was my subconscious way of blaming Clete for riding his bike that day.

That upset me, because I don't feel I ever did blame him. Any guilt or blame I've always attached to myself, however irrational that may be. It all comes back to the feeling that I could always protect him from everything, if only I was good enough.

I guess Alta is correct about being careful what I wish for, because so far none of my dreams have been very good ones. ~

Finding Grace

I just finished John Ortberg's book *Love Beyond Reason.* It has given me much to ponder.

Yesterday, as I left Higher Grounds, I walked over to sit in the chapel at St. Mark's Church. It is small and private. As I sat there and thought about this feeling that Clete's soul is not at rest, I wept. I prayed for God to find an answer for me.

One of the insights that came to me is this. There is a parallel in how I could never quite forgive my father for how he treated my mother, until finally I realized that this put a hold on me I did not want.

The hurt this would do to Clete is hard for me to let go. I am putting on my shoulders a burden that is not mine. Certainly, if he were alive, he would be deeply hurt. But he is not, and so I am coming closer to believing his soul is at peace. Somehow I must make it not my problem to live with, but theirs to be at peace with if they ever have the insight to see it.

One of the great things about Ortberg's books is his use of humor to illustrate a point. In a section in *Love Beyond Reason* called "Practicing Gratitude," he relates this story about how parents from time immemorial have asked their children what they say when someone gives them a gift or does them a favor:

"What do you say to Aunt Eva for her Velveeta, Spam, and lima bean casserole?" my parents would ask me.

How's a kid supposed to respond?

It was not really a question. They'd have been surprised if I'd said, "Aunt Eva, what in the name of heaven were you thinking? Aunt Eva, you should not be allowed to prepare meals—someone should put you away."

I especially liked his chapter on love and grace. He writes that grace-providers simply never cease to love you. They see beneath the surface; they see the darkness as well as the goodness in your heart. I would add, to be touched by grace as well as being able to dispense grace is surely a God moment.

I laughed when I read this story as he was illustrating grace: "Not long ago in my marriage, one of the two of us wanted for us to take dancing lessons. The other one of us said yes, because that one is a gracious person, and because it was a way of earning bonus points; kind of like matrimonial frequent flier miles that can be cashed in later." ~

Where Am I Now?

It is more than sixteen months since he died—where am I now? That is a question I really have to think about.

The week of the Fourth of July was terrible. It would have been our fifty-fifth anniversary. I went to my hide-a-way, but that did not help much.

Still, as I think back, I want to try and remember the positive things. The gift that was given to me as I reached the hospital in time to speak to him, however short that time was. The strength and conviction it took to see that he was well cared for. The ability and courage and love that it took to grant his last wish—to allow him to go as gently as possible into that dark night.

To be able to lie in bed with him one last time, to kiss his cheek and calm him when they took him off the ventilator, to sing to him and keep touching him as his breathing was so labored. When I was told his brain was shut down, I believe he knew that I was there trying to protect him until the very end.

So where am I now? I am still very sad, still miss him more than words can describe. Physically, I am exhausted much of the time. When one is alone there is too much and sometimes not enough time to think. That sounds like an oxymoron. As I search for a way across these slippery slopes, I sometimes make problems where they do not exist. That is getting better.

I have been able to travel, and on the whole that has been good. It was also a huge step forward for me. I miss him terribly when I want to have an intelligent conversation with someone about politics or books, or even to have a spirited discussion with someone on something we disagree about. His wit, his smile, his unconditional love are there no more.

I am very much wanting that person back in my world who cared about me, who protected me, who I could depend on to take care of me. That is gone forever.

On my good days I am very much looking forward to a trip to Ireland in September. On my terrible days, I can't imagine how I will do it and yet I very much want to.

Some of the things I have had to do are very empowering. I marvel that I can possibly do them—both physically and mentally. My ability to deal with all the financial and insurance problems is a testament to how well he treated me: as an equal, and a smart one at that.

The other day, when I took down some birdhouses and a ten-foot pole one was mounted on, I stood down in the wetlands soaking wet with sweat as I thought, by God, I did it!

Bethany came later that week and weed-whacked the wetlands. She helped me carry the stuff up to load into her Jeep to get rid of it at her place. That was great.

I am blessed with great friends who are a wonderful support system for me—still, nothing takes the place of the soul mate I had shared my life with since I was seventeen years old.

I do count my blessings because at my last eye check-up I had no serious problems, and at my dermatologist appointment I needed nothing taken off for the first time in a long time. I adore Dr. Kegel and we laughed as I told her some Clete stories. I survived my stress-cardio test that took only two and a half hours instead of the four hours I thought it would take.

My fears—well, the worst one is that if I have serious health problems I will have no one to care for me. I am trying to figure out a game plan if that were to happen. I was excited to read about the Lancaster General Hospital's new rehabilitation wing. That would sure beat going to a nursing home for rehab.

One of the greatest gifts is that we moved into the townhouse nine years before he died. I love this place and feel very safe here, on my good days very much at peace and close to him. He loved this place. That can be both a blessing and a curse. Saturday evenings are hard when I think of how often at the end of the day we would shower and flop down onto our bed (always sunny at that time of the day) and decide where we would go to eat and talk about our day.

I don't think I am quite as hard on myself as I was at the beginning. Only a fool would not have regrets, but I do see that in the things that really mattered we were always there for each other.

In some ways I am better and in some ways I am not. The realization that never again on this earth will that figure coming toward me be him, that couple walking holding hands will not be us, the couple laughing and talking at a coffee shop are so fortunate—but they are not Nan and Clete. Never, ever again.

Those are the days when I want to shout, "I want another chance! I want to live our life all over again and get it really right." Of course, even in my brokenness I realize that would be a very sterile, boring life.

Our life was not perfect, but oh, in so many ways it was absolutely glorious. How smart I was to marry that man! ~

Random Thoughts
and Happenings

I was sitting on the deck the other day, feeling at peace for a change and thinking I felt happy. I sort of gasped and thought, Oh no, I can't feel happy! Now what, I wonder, was that all about? Do I feel that I have no right to be happy since Clete is not here? Is that what is keeping me so down, so unsettled? I just do not know.

So here I am, still feeling crappy a lot of the time. Perhaps a lot of it has to do with having no one to share just the everyday things with.

A few days ago while I was riding my bike and not paying attention to my shifting, my chain ring popped off. Believe me, it is not as easy to get back on as it was on my Terry bike. This bike weighs a ton and I cannot lift it to easily get the chain back on. After a fifteen-minute struggle, working with my nails newly manicured, getting grease on my fingers down to the middle knuckle, and getting one of Clete's pure white hankies good and greasy, I succeeded.

Today while riding I foolishly decided to cut across to another road where the pavement was not even. I stopped to lift my bike, did not get my one foot out of the toe clip, and had what I call a lean over. Other people call them falls. I went down on my left side fairly hard. Nothing was broken but when I went to get back on my bike I realized my seat was badly askew. Of course I couldn't straighten it, because I do not have the strength in my hands to loosen the quick release (that's an oxymoron if I ever heard one). So I rode that last three-quarters of a mile with the seat poking me in my left thigh. I decided I would see if I could find some tools in Clete's bike tool box to grip the quick release and fix the seat. Success! Another hurdle crossed.

Then I started to cry—my body hurt, I wanted my Clete to be there to tell about it. He would have said, "Oh, honey, come here, you need a hug. Good job. I'll go check the bike to make sure everything is OK."

I don't think I'll ever get used to not having him here to tell about my foibles and misadventures. If I would tell that story to my daughters they would say, good for you. That is not what I want to hear. I just want someone to say, what a bummer. ~

"People who don't take themselves too seriously give a great gift to those around them. In contrast, joy-challenged people face a serious handicap in trying to live in community."

John Ortberg, *Everybody's Normal Till You Get to Know Them*

Who Am I Going to Become?

"We have two women who assume how the other feels and thinks. How do two people bridge such a gap? What does it take to give up expectations of what another person ought to be, or say, or do?"

From the question section of
At Home in Covington by Joan Medlicott

The character is a forty something man who has lost his wife to cancer and is bereft. Months after her death, he completely falls apart.

"He walked over to the bed and fell back on it, gazing up to the ceiling. Keep thinking — that's it — keep thinking. What the hell do you want, David?

I want to be — alone!" he said out loud, "just — unknown! I don't particularly want to be — David — [@#^$%*&] — Corstorphine — any bloody more!"

From *An Ocean Apart*,
a novel by Robin Pilcher

I use these two quotes because I think they say a lot about how far I've come and how far I have to go.

At the very beginning I said I feel like I am in a foreign country where people speak a different language and I don't know if I will ever learn that language or like this foreign land.

Of terrible necessity I learned to negotiate this land, with all its back streets and people with different customs. The language of insurance speak, lawyer speak, financial planner speak, the being responsible for handling all the money aspect, balancing accounts, seeing tax accountants. Medicare, all the aspects of straightening out the intricacies that come with an accidental death. Coming to grips with the frightening knowledge that even the experts do not always have the correct answers.

This can be one of the most exhausting things one has to deal with. Particularly if you must do it alone. As early as four months after Clete's death, I was left to fend for myself. There's a certain feeling of "well done," that I learned to manage all that. At the same time, it sapped my strength and energy.

It is now seventeen months since Clete's death and I feel as though I have mastered most of it—that I can finally sit back and breathe. In addition, one of the most helpful parts of the healing process is now at an end: serving on the search committee for a new pastor at church.

At this point I took a break and went out to ride bike. I'm close to turning over seven hundred miles on my odometer and 100 miles for this month so far. That is a lot for me.

As I went up onto a part of the school project that is not yet finished, I almost wiped out on some gravel. Due to my superior bike-handling abilities (oh yeah, right!) I managed to stay upright. So maybe the question of who will take care of me will be answered in a heartbeat and I can fly to heaven to be with Clete. God alone knows what is in store for me, and I think I like it that way.

After lunch I went up to the grave site. I kicked my shoes off and sat on the grass in front of the tombstone. I started crying and talked to Clete. I told him I plan to go to Ireland and asked him if he was OK with that. I told him I am afraid of who I will become—to find a life without him seems like a betrayal. It is as though I feel I do not deserve to be happy.

I can see that this phase is progress, and yet it is going to be hard, slow going. ~

"Let me hear the sounds of joy and gladness; and though you have crushed me and broken me, I will be happy once again."

Psalm 51:8 (TEV)

Dear Dr. Saylor

Dear Dr. Saylor,

As I have been riding my bicycle this summer, I often go through the new middle school property—a wonderful, safe shortcut out to White Oak Road.

When Clete died, we were presented an American flag at the grave site because he was an Army veteran. It suddenly occurred to me that it would be a wonderful memorial to Clete if it would fly over the new middle school.

Two days before his accident, on a Saturday morning, we were taking our usual walk around Lititz, very near to where he had his accident. I was commenting on how well he was doing after all the surgical procedures in the previous ten months. He had stopped delivering the mail for the district during that time because of lifting restrictions. He mentioned to me that he thought he would like to resume delivering the mail.

At first I was taken aback and not too happy about that. Then I thought, what is this really about? The answer was that he loved his job, and loved the people. He missed doing the mail because he missed the people. It was only a few months until his retirement. I told him that it was OK with me if he wanted to do that, but I wanted him to wait another week until he saw Dr. Del Terzo, his urologist. He was due to be checked to see if he was still cancer free.

He truly loved working for Manheim Central. He often said it was the best job he ever had. I think he thought about retirement with mixed emotions. He would be very pleased and proud to have his flag fly over the new school. I have only one request if you accept this gift. I would like to be present the first time they raise the flag.

Please let me know if you would accept my offer.

Sincerely,
Nan Gibble

The school did accept my offer. It was a very moving ceremony. They only flew his flag for one day, then I presented it to the school in a wooden triangular case along with a picture and a copy of what I wrote for the dedication. They put it in the case in the lobby along with the other school trophies. I was very touched. ~

A Prisoner in My Own Home

For three days I have been held hostage in my own home by Medicare. Again the insurance industry is making my life a living hell. Again I am left to deal with it by myself. For who would help me?

I wonder how Clete would be doing if the roles were reversed. He would be handling the finances with more assurance and confidence. With the health insurance, he would not do so well, because that was my job.

This time I simply do know how to solve this problem. They insisted they are not my primary insurer when in fact they now are. They promised to call me back in forty-eight hours. Well, unless they call in twenty minutes, that time frame's gone. If anything would put me over the edge it would be this endless dealing with insurance companies. At least if Clete were alive we would be doing it together. Well, I'd be doing it and he would be listening halfheartedly and being not much help. But at least he would be here.

I do not like to have to deal with my providers, although I am sure they are far more used to it then I am. More's the pity.

It is this sort of thing that makes me extremely depressed and hopeless. I'm tired, I'm lonely, I'm exhausted, and I physically hurt. My heart is broken; I don't think even one little piece of it is mended. If I could only lie down and sleep a deep sleep for forty-eight hours straight, maybe I could deal with life again. I never in a million years thought I would be so abandoned. Life is what happens when you are not paying attention.

Maybe I'll just say the heck with it and leave the chips fall where they may and hope it all somehow works out.

So much for this pity party. ~

"When you get into a tight place, and everything goes against you till it seems as if you couldn't hold on a minute longer, never give up then, for that's just the place and time that the tide'll turn."

Harriet Beecher Stowe

Rock Bottom

After five long days on the telephone to Medicare or waiting on hold or just waiting for them to call me, I am exhausted and worn out. I finally got through today and think I got it fixed.

Then another call to my supplemental insurance had me in tears.

For over a year I have been dealing with insurance and I am worn out. One of my insurance people told me I shouldn't even have to bother myself about this.

How nice that sounds, and how untrue. If I had not, I would constantly be denied coverage under Medicare. Pray tell, who else is going to fix it? Now I will trust the rest will come together.

I do not want to be the "fixer." I want someone else to worry about these problems—to be in control. To take care of insurance and bills and finances. To worry if the money will last, to take care of me if I am unfortunate enough to be incapacitated. It is all just too hard. I feel no joy in life and very seldom do I feel peace. Everything is just too hard.

I do not want to burden my dear friends with all of this. They have done so much.

I weep as I write this. Life should not have to be this hard.

I want to forget it all, to go back in time. Or perhaps forward in time when I will be with Clete again. ~

Your Mind Rejects What Is Too Painful to See

Last week, after I came home from Ireland, Jackie and I went to the Fulton to see *West Side Story*.

As we were on our way to eat at the Prince Street Cafe, I noticed that there was a car crosswise at the entrance to the Prince Street garage. Traffic was very slow and I saw a girl standing there and a bicycle that had obviously been hit. The front wheel was all bent. As we passed I saw another girl on a cell phone looking out into the street; behind her, lying on the ground, was a man flat on his back. He was moving his legs and rubbing his head. I saw no blood. I told Jackie, "Oh, I should stop," but I could not do so safely without causing another accident. Jackie rubbed my leg and said, "You didn't need to see that. She must be calling for an ambulance." We went on to the Hager Street lot, parked, and went in to eat at the cafe.

I kind of put it out of my mind, but during the play it bothered me as I wondered if he was OK.

Thursday night at about 1:30 A.M. I got awake and could not get back to sleep. I kept seeing the man in my mind and feeling absolutely terrible that I did not go back. The sight of him rubbing his head brought back terrible memories of Clete's accident. The fact that I did not at least go see if I could do anything, talk to him and give him comfort, bothered me terribly. I kept thinking of all the people who had helped Clete that awful day. I know there were people there and they were calling for help, but the thought that no one was touching him and comforting him sent me into a deep panic and depression.

I almost called Alta that morning. I did not have the Thursday paper to see if there was anything in it about the accident. There was nothing in the Friday paper. When I got to work I told Jackie I needed to talk to her as soon as we were done with the mail. I told her about my concerns. She said she saw an ambulance go past not long after we were sitting down. That made me feel so much better.

Still, I beat myself up. I thought back to when I was in Ireland. A few of us were standing in a little square-like island in the middle of a big city when suddenly I heard what sounded like a gunshot. I turned around and saw that a man had collapsed on the sidewalk and was bleeding badly from his head. I went over and knelt down to help him. He was talking as I got some tissues out of my purse to try to stop the bleeding. He was obviously three sheets to the wind. I told him not to try to get up and tried to calm him as I still tried to stop the bleeding. A police woman showed up, said an ambulance was coming. It seemed to take forever.

Finally the ambulance came and took over. By that time a small crowd had gathered and I was standing there with my hands covered in blood. I walked over to the ambulance to see if they had anything I could clean my hands with. They did not. Go figure. There were a group of young American guys standing there. They started pulling wet wipes out of their backpacks for me to clean my hands as they told me they were back-packing through Europe. I laughed and asked how their parents felt about that. They replied that they only had to call home once a week anymore instead of every day.

I handled that and was OK but went into a post-traumatic episode about the gentleman in Lancaster. What was the difference? On reflection I think it was because I could actually try to comfort and help this man, while no one was actually touching the other gentleman.

It brought back all the bad memories. The feelings of if only I had done this or done that, going back to the terrible ten months before the accident. Even when one knows better, one has a tendency to want to play God. ~

"Where God goes, hope grows."

Edward Grinnan, *Daily Guideposts*

The Things I Want to Remember

OK, here are some of the things I want to fill my mind with about our life together as I try to roust the demons from my brain about the accident:

I loved him.

He loved me.

I liked the way he would smile at me, the way in church he would sometimes take my hand and hold it.

Walking down the street and holding hands, the many, many walks we took together. It was good talking time with no interruptions.

Training Misha, our Lab retriever. What a challenge, but good memories too. Walking out a neighbors lane with the Mish and being able to let him loose. I can still see the day he came running back towards us and I could see he was heading straight for a mud puddle. I am yelling, "No, Mish, no!" But sure enough, he went right through it and joyously jumped right up on me, making me muddy from head to toe. Clete and I stood there and laughed and laughed.

The time we were sitting on the back porch talking one afternoon and I said to him, I guess you want to go for a bike ride. He said, no, he didn't, he wanted to stay and talk to me. That was special because he was really interested in our conversation.

The Sunday afternoons after checking our dresser drawers to see if we could come up with enough money to take the children for ice cream cones at Good's Dairy Bar. They had the best mint chocolate chip ice cream. We'd drive over and sit at their picnic tables enjoying our cones. We all still love Coleman's mint chocolate chip. Nothing like it!

I soon learned to say, when I asked him where he went for a ride, I just meant the general direction. His mind was like one of those systems in cars that tell you exactly what street to turn, how many miles to the next turn, etc., etc., etc. He kept a bike log and coded his favorite routes. At his death, Matt looked at his log and could tell what his route had been that day, just by checking his previous logs.

For years we had always gone out to eat on Friday night. I always worked Fridays. In the last year or two of his life, when he was putting in long days in the school van, driving in all kinds of weather, and I was stressed out from another day at the Auction, we'd look at each other and say, what do you think? We'd kind of both decide we would rather stay in than go out again in the cold or rainy weather.

He even stopped going down to high school football games. He stayed home and watched them on TV. We just liked being down in the family room in front of the fireplace all cozy and warm. He often would come over and give me a hug. We just liked being together.

All our wonderful vacations—the Bahamas, Switzerland, Italy, London and the English countryside, Vermont, Prince Edward Island, Colorado, the seventeen-day trip to the Pacific Northwest, San Diego, the Grand Canyon, Arizona, and many more. We would sometimes think, can we afford this? Well, we always went, and what grand adventures we had. ~

Misha was a valued member of our family for twelve years. Clete adored him and would sometimes put him on the leash, get on his bike, and ride out a country lane close to our home. "The Mish" would get so excited, I think Clete could hardly keep up. For that reason, I share this story published in the Lancaster Sunday News *on October 29, 2000.*

I KNOW A STORY

Misha's last grand adventure

By Nancy Garner Gibble
Special to the Sunday News

Once upon a time, a Man and a Lady went to visit a vineyard. There they saw two wonderful laid-back yellow Labrador Retrievers.

"Wouldn't it be a fine thing," said the Lady, "to get one of those fine, gentle dogs?"

Now the Man looked at the Lady as though she had just grown two heads.

"Why would we want to do that? We are what some might call senior age. All of our children except the 23-year-old son are gone, and you were never much of a dog person."

"True," said the Lady, "but I take long walks, and how nice it would be to have a companion."

So it came to pass that the Man and the Lady and the Son brought home a beautiful Lab puppy and they named him Misha. Soon reality set in, as they discovered Lab puppies, while beautiful, loving and devoted, are also headstrong, energetic and strong. To school the puppy and the Man and the Son went—once, twice, three times—and eventually the puppy grew into a fine, handsome, obedient (most of the time) dog.

Now the handsome Misha kept the Man and the Lady's home safe. He tolerated squirrels but chased off cats and rabbits. He had bizarre accidents and was five times attacked by other dogs—never once winning a fight. In short, the handsome Misha led a rather checkered life.

Eventually Misha was border-trained, spending much time in his large back yard. So it was in disbelief the Lady looked at the good Neighbor when he told her the handsome Misha was seen running down their busy country road.

The Lady and the Dog had taken many walks into the sleepy little town a mile and a half away. They would go along that busy road and onto another, even busier one, cut into a development, to reach the town. There, they would walk along the streets, crossing intersections and a railroad track until they came to the business that the Man owned.

If the Man wasn't too busy, the handsome Dog would get a pat on the head and an ear-scratching, and the Lady might get a kiss. On the way home, they would stop at the little corner store for the daily paper, a cup of coffee and a cheese Danish, then on to the gazebo in the middle of the sleepy little town's square to relax for a bit before they headed home.

Distraught at news of the Dog's escape, the Lady called the Man and they started in separate cars to search for Misha. As the Lady drove into the town, she was sure she might see the Dog sitting in the gazebo having a cup of coffee, a cheese Danish and reading the paper. Alas, he had no money.

Confident that Misha had simply taken the familiar walk without her, she drove on. When she arrived at the Man's business, there sat the wayward Dog in the office, patiently waiting, with a look that clearly said, "What took you so long?"

That was a very long time ago. Misha is now an old dog, no longer able to go on those long walks with his Lady.

But sometimes when the Lady is sitting on her patio having her coffee and reading a book while her Dog lies in the sun, she will glance up and see him lift his head, sniff the air and get a faraway look in his eyes. And the Lady just knows he is remembering that long-ago day when he flew down that busy country road and into the sleepy little town.

Then Misha will give a little sigh as he puts his head down between his paws and thinks, "Oh, but that was a grand adventure!"

And the Lady smiles and goes back to reading her book.

The Author

This is the third story by Nancy Garner Gibble, Manheim, to be published in "I Know a Story."

She is married to Cletus L. Gibble, the "Man" in the story. They have four grown children, but share their home with Misha.

Mrs. Gibble works part-time at the Manheim Auto Auction, reads, writes, takes long walks, and has tutored a student in English as a second language.

Someday, Oh Someday

I figured out why it's so hard to go to my home church around any holiday. Everyone asks me what I am going to be doing. If I say I will be alone, the "look" comes into their eyes because they feel sorry for me. I do not want people to feel sorry for me. Better alone than masquerading as something I am not.

I think this winter may be worse than last year. Maybe not. I put on some old records this morning and during one of the songs—it was so poignant and beautiful, it mirrored my feelings about losing Clete so well—I sat there and wept and wept. They were cleansing tears and I needed them. There's still such a great hole in my heart.

I try to hold on to the image of him whole and well, no drops to put in his eyes, no constant doctor appointments, no side effects from all the medications he was on, not another cataract operation, no every-three-month scope of his bladder to make sure he was cancer free.

He does fly free now and for that I should be forever grateful.

I want to set you free, Darling, but I feel as though I want to hold on to the kite string that sent you soaring. Do you remember when we were out with Matt and you and he put a kite up? It flew so high that none of us could see it, or just barely. It was a magical moment for us all. You are that kite and I can no longer see you— but someday, oh someday. ~

The Second Anniversary and Beyond

It seems like a long time since I have written anything. Much has happened since Christmas. I feel as though I am finally becoming stronger, yet events continue to show me how fragile I still am.

I got up on the twentieth and was at the breakfast table finishing my devotional readings and trying to decide what I wanted to do with this day when the phone rang. It was my dear friend Marti, whom I had gone to Savannah with last May. I had not heard from her in quite some time. She and I talked for probably close to an hour. We laughed and reminisced about Clete. We cried. She shared that she thinks of him often and in her own marriage she now tries to remember that the small irritations do not matter. It was exactly the contact I needed to start my two-day mourning period.

It was a gloomy day but I forced myself to go down to Annie Bailey's Irish Cafe for a late lunch. That was a good decision. It was completely deserted except for me and the wait staff. I found a cozy place to sit, had a leisurely lunch, chatted with the staff a bit, and thoroughly enjoyed myself.

On the twenty-first I went down to the hospital in the early afternoon. I had lunch in the cafe and, as always, felt at peace being in the last place I saw him alive. I wandered over to the gift shop and stocked up on their marvelous greeting cards. Then, as I usually do, I bought something outlandishly expensive. This year's buy was a black leather purse with brightly colored ribbons decorating it. It makes me smile to look at it.

I then got another latte and went up to the second floor where I'd spent so much time two years ago, sat in a quiet corner, and thought about all that has transpired in these last two years. I had a newspaper and saw that his memorial was in the evening paper. I tore it out, went back down to the gift shop, picked out some flowers, attached one of the cards I had just bought, wrote a note inside, and enclosed his memorial. The gift shop took care of delivering it to the neurotrauma unit for me.

I do not know if that is the right thing to do for the staff, but for me it is marvelously healing. When things get very bad, it helps to go back and thank God for all the blessings Clete and I received right from the very beginning. To know that he was well cared for and to be surrounded by all that love and caring is an experience I will never forget—nor do I want to.

I had lit a memorial candle at 6 P.M. on the twentieth, and on the twenty-first by the time I got home I was very tired, but feeling peace. I needed to get a shower and picked up the candle to take up to the bathroom with me as it was close to six o'clock, the time of his death.

I went down to the rec room with my candle still burning. All in all I can see that I am making progress even though I still miss him more than words can say.

The memorial candle burned thirty hours and six minutes, the longest it has ever burned. He lived for exactly thirty hours after the accident. I consider my little candle burning so long this year a great gift. ~

A Topsy-Turvy World

I do feel that the last two weeks I have been so busy that I am living in a topsy-turvy world. A lot of good things have happened, but I still feel not right in my skin.

The odd thing is that after a really nice evening with my friend Kathy and her family, I woke the next morning oddly depressed.

Why is that, I wonder? It has happened before. I will have a special time and the next day feel very down.

I had to again deal with some financial issues and walked out of Paul's office wanting to smack him. After some advice from Sam and thinking things through by myself, I decided to go with my own instincts and then I felt better. I really, really, really hate dealing with that stuff.

Sam was a sweetheart though. He came up to see what was wrong with my new answering machine setup, agreed that it just wasn't right, took it out, went and exchanged it, came back and set up a new one for me. He then talked to me about my financial concerns.

The best part, however, was that after we did all that stuff, he just sat and talked to me about Clete. We talked about the day of the accident and his death. He is the only one in Pennsylvania who has really sat and talked to me about those days and how he felt about it all. It was very special and I loved him for it.

I also booked a trip to Amsterdam, Luxembourg, and Brussels for September 12th through the 21st. I would have liked to wait to book later, but I guess it is good I didn't, because some of the flights were full.

I told my friend Sandra, who is from Austria, about the trip and she said, "Oh, you're young, go ahead and do it." I told her she's my new best friend.

I find myself at times feeling very irritable, however—very tired of people complaining about nitpicky things. Don't ask me why, since I certainly do that myself.

I was talking to a friend whose husband died. She asked how I was doing and I said, better. She remarked that it's hard but that you get over it—you have to. Well, I don't agree with that. I don't think I will ever "get over it." Nor do I want to. I want to be better, I do not want this grief to consume me, but get "over it"? No, I do not want that to happen. To let that happen would seem to do a great disservice to both Clete and me and what our life together meant.

I do realize that, in spite of all the ups and downs, ours was a special marriage and I am one of the luckiest women in the world to have known him. Did I appreciate that every day of every year of our marriage? Of course not; nor did he. We were not fools. But as hard as that last year was, I hope he still realized that we had the best there was, and a great life. ~

Ah-Ha Moments

My sessions with Alta are always the best parts of my life. Sometimes I experience a real ah-ha moment. Such a moment happened on Monday. We were talking about my becoming a deacon in my church and the responsibilities it entails. She asked me what Clete would think about all this, what he would say.

I said he would be supportive and proud. Then I had my ah-ha moment—because, in truth, if he were still alive, I would not be doing this. I had thought that after he retired, he and I would finally have a life all our own to do exactly what we wanted. I had no illusions that it would be perfect; certainly it would be an adjustment as we discovered how to live together with no big responsibilities. We would have looked for volunteer opportunities—he probably for a part-time job a day or two a week. Of course I am still working; he would have looked forward to those days I was out of the house. I knew his health was failing and I felt a certain sadness that the days of really extensive travel were over.

I was looking forward to waking up in the morning with him beside me—to lazing around and talking sleepily. There is not a lovely day that passes that I do not think how much he would love being out on his bike. It breaks my heart that this man who had been working since the age of twelve does not have this time to do exactly what he wants. Maybe we would have gone to some elder hostels. The possibilities were endless.

It was then I realized that this is the first step in making a new life for myself, a life without him: doing something I would never have considered had he lived. I did not want any more heavy responsibilities.

The pain is still great; even this morning I sat at the breakfast table and wept. I think I will forever have those times. But—and this is a big but—since I seem destined to be on this earth for a longer time, I have moved to where I realize I have to somehow find a place for myself, doing something that gives some kind of meaning to my life. He still influences me greatly in the fact that there is little I do without wondering what he would think of it.

In just everyday things I do not always do things the way he did. He's no longer here and I do them the way I want; still, I always weigh the pros and cons of different decisions. I am not as impetuous as I was; I think things through longer and that is a good thing. He was a good example in many things. He also could drive me crazy in lots of ways. That, of course, is what marriage is all about.

I really wonder about people who never complain about their spouses. Oh, not the big important things, of course. Those are private and it would be a betrayal to do that. But the everyday little irritations—surely everyone has some.

One of my favorite jokes was that one does not break up a marriage because of another woman, but because of the way he chews his pretzels!

Music continues to speak to me. It has been one of the most healing things. I can cry buckets of tears over a song, but I can also see our marriage in many of the lyrics.

There is one called the *Birthday Song*, sung by Helen Reddy, from the 1970s that I have been playing lately and I love it. I especially love these verses:

You see I love the way you love me
Love the way you smile at me
I love the way we live this life we're in
I don't believe in magic
But I do believe in you
And when you say believe in me
There's so much magic I can do

So, my darling, for the magical life we lived, for your smile, and for your love of me through the best and the worst of times, thank you. I wouldn't change a thing. ~

Reflections

Hi darling, it's me, Nan.

It's been two and one half years that you are gone. I am not handling it very well.

What would we do if we had one more week together? Would we waste it on regrets? I hope not, as I've done that endlessly the last two years. As I spoke of this to Alta, she softly said, "Then you would lose him again." That hit home.

I think this will be really a hodgepodge of thoughts. You will be delighted to know I bought a little light-weight cleaner that is much easier on my back. It does stairs nicely and the upstairs carpets. Now I only have to kill myself once a month when I give the place a good going over.

~ August 13, 2008 ~

OK, this is one of the things I miss. Having you here to talk to about absolutely unimportant things. It almost makes me laugh when I think how much time I have spent thinking "what if" and "if only," when in truth I can never get our life back. However, I can take pleasure in the life we had. Not just the huge wonderful mountain-top times, and we certainly had those, but the everyday average times. The knowing that you were always there—to talk to, laugh with, argue with, be silly with— my rock in a crazy world. It is the terrible, terrible loneliness, the absolute finality of it all. The last week or so I have been feeling more at peace than I have for a while. Still, when I have a sort of "good day," I am just as quickly down and sad the next. To quote a book I read, "I am waiting for peace—an end of my own personal warfare." When, if ever, will that come? I wonder.

~ August 14, 2008 ~

Remember when we ran ambulance? I think those were some of our most rewarding years. I started laughing today as I remembered the time a call came in and I was the only one who showed up at the garage. It was for an auto accident down by Krieder's on Route 72. As you know, I never drove the ambulance, by choice. However, I decided in this case I was going to have to and prayed some crew members would be at the scene. Of course I had to drive right by your gas station. You knew there was a call from listening to your scanner. I will never forget the look on your face as I barreled down Main Street. When I got to the scene the police were there; you were following me in your pickup truck and some other crew members showed up. I wish I had a picture of your look of astonishment when you saw me driving. I do—don't I?—forever in my heart. What a life! I love you.

~ August 17, 2008 ~

Several months ago, in one of my low times, I wrote this in a quote book: "The waiting time—move from the past, what's in the future? A time to be silent and wait and see what is in store, a very frightening time for I do not want to move on for fear I will lose you all over again."

I am like a cat in a room full of rocking chairs—on edge, irritable, physically a mess.

Right now I am a bit better and more at ease. It is just such a long rocky road. I call myself and some of my friends who are going through these hard times "the walking wounded." We function but are not quite in this world. It is very rocky.

Matt and I have been talking a lot these last few days since his hernia surgery. He is funny and it is as if I am talking to you. I told him the story of when we were in the house on Hosler Road before we remodeled the kitchen. He barely remembers that.

I was looking for something and could not find it (shades of today). We were standing in the middle of the kitchen and you said, "Nan, it's right over there on top of the refrigerator." I still could not see it and you were slightly exasperated. I walked across the kitchen and put my nose up against the refrigerator, which was a good foot or more above the top of my head. "Oh, you are short." Well, either I was short or the refrigerator was very large. Of course, you were almost six feet tall to my five feet five inches.

~ September 1, 2008 ~

I am getting ready to go to Europe, Amsterdam, Luxembourg, and Brussels. I hate getting bills paid, getting dollars changed into Euros, thinking about what to pack. That is pretty easy though since I can only have one bag and have finally gotten smart enough not to overpack. I'll be glad when I am on the plane in Harrisburg and especially in Philadelphia. Then I can relax and just enjoy the ride. I'll think of you a lot when I am there, but in a more peaceful way.

In the beginning Pat Hart said that one day I will realize I have not thought about you at all that day and will feel very, very, guilty. So far that has not happened. Not a day goes by that I don't think of you. ~

Dear Ben

Dear Ben,

I've been thinking about you a lot as you turn thirteen. It is the third Christmas without your Grandpa. I thought I would write you a letter and tell you some Grandpa stories.

Since you and your Dad started hunting it reminded me of Clete going out small game hunting and deer hunting when we were first married. At that time he could walk out our back door and bag a couple of rabbits and maybe a pheasant. He had to clean them and maybe I would cook them. I did not like game meat.

When he was a boy he often went out with his Dad. He had a beagle dog that he trained to hunt. He told me the story of when he was hunting with this dog with his Dad and his Dad's friends. They observed how well the dog did and said to Grandpa, "That's some dog you've got there, boy." That was high praise in those days.

After we married, he had a pair of beagles that we kept outside. One time he let them out of their pen and they ran off. They took off over the fields and hills and Grandpa walked all the way to Sporting Hill, as far as Mt. Joy Road, before he could catch those little rebels. I don't think I have ever seen your Grandpa so angry. Another time, during a snowstorm we decided we would bring them into the basement because it was too cold and windy to have them outside. Well, those rascals got ahold of my high school field hockey jacket and chewed the cuffs right off of it. I was not too happy about that because it was the only school jacket I could afford to buy when I was in school. I kind of think he gave up on hunting dogs after that.

He hunted white-tailed dear for many years. The year your Dad and Mom got married, Clete and Matt went up to Dry Holler Camp for what was to be their last hunt together. That would have been in 1991, if I am correct. As you know, hunters tell their story again and again and again, but this was a special one. I do not know which one got their deer first, but within five minutes the other one shot a deer. Your Dad and Grandpa looked at each other and just laughed and laughed and laughed. Grandpa never hunted again after that. He told me that nothing could top that experience of standing in the mountains with his son and having such a great hunt.

Now here is a tip for when you get married. I soon learned how quickly I got tired of hearing the same hunting story over and over. Finally, one year I told Grandpa, "I will listen to your story once with interest, once more out of politeness, and then I NEVER want to hear it again!" Worked out pretty well for both of us.

Grandpa lived a much different life than you do. When he was twelve his parents sent him to a farm right outside of Manheim to work for a farmer for the summer. Grandpa would stay there all week, get his meals with the family, and I think he was paid the grand sum of somewhere between $2.00 to $4.00 a week. Then on the weekend he would go home. These were not just eight-hour days. He learned at an early age the value of hard work and doing a job well. His next joy was working at Linn Longenecker's greenhouse helping with the flowers.

Grandpa always liked sports. He went out for summer baseball. The coach told him he was good in the field but

could not hit worth a darn. I think he played basketball also. However, after his father died, when Grandpa was sixteen, he dropped out of all sports so he could get a job and help his mother with the bills. Your Grandpa never complained about very much. He just did what he had to do. He was really special in that way.

After he graduated from high school he worked in a factory for a short period and then found work as a mechanic. I think he liked that work, but he had his ambitions. Neither of us ever considered the idea of college because our mothers simply could not afford to send us.

He never dated much but ran around with a group of guys. They liked to drive their cars fast and do some hijinks. He and about four other guys took a trip to Florida together. I think they drove in two cars. One night they were driving too fast and a police car started chasing them. They did not want to get caught because the driver's license had been suspended. They took that police car on a merry chase through several small Florida towns. The officer radioed ahead and finally they were caught and stopped. "Boys, that's a mighty fast car, but not as fast as a police radio."

I think they had also been throwing fire crackers out of the window of the car. Anyway, the officer wanted to know who was driving and no one would own up. They had decided among them who would be the fall guy if worse came to worst. Finally the officer said, "Boys, one of you better 'fess up or you're all going to jail." I think Grandpa took the blame (although he was not driving). The officer did let them all go.

When Grandpa told me that story on a trip to Florida in the early 1990s I said, good heavens, Clete, I always thought you were such a good guy. I had to laugh at his stories, although I did say that if his boys had done any of that stuff he would have had a fit. (Of course they did do their share.) When we told Aunt Bethany that story, she asked her Dad if he had been drinking. He said, "Oh no, I never drank"—and he never did.

Grandpa was a great guy and a lot of fun. He had a great sense of humor and was very smart. He had ambitions to be more then just a mechanic, although there is nothing wrong with that job. He really wanted to own his own business and in the late 1950s he opened his own gas station/repair shop at the lower end of Manheim. He was very successful and it gave us a good living until we had a gas leak in the early 1990s and had to close the business. He then went to work for the school district and loved it.

I guess this is a long enough letter for this time. Just always remember how much your MeMa and Grandpa love you, and always try to do your best. Sometimes you'll make mistakes or do things you are sorry for. That is OK, we all do that; the key is to try to do better the next time.

I love you, Ben, and wish your Grandpa was still here. I know we would be coming out to Colorado in the winter to see you participate in sports. I'm just glad you knew grandpa for ten years and I hope you will always remember him.

Love, MeMa ~

If I Had to Choose

If I had to chose just one day / to last my whole life through / it would surely be that Sunday / the day that I met you*

It was actually a Saturday. You offered Sally and me a ride home from the movies in Lancaster, four guys picking up two girls. We were all from the same town and it was safe to do that then.

Newborn Whip-poor-wills were callin' from the hills / Summer was a comin' in but fast / Lots of daffodils were showin' off their skills / nodding all together I could almost hear them whisper / go on kiss him, go on and kiss him.

It was fall that was a comin' and a day or two later you called and asked me for our first date—a movie date. I remember sitting in the theater beside you and thinking, "He's the nicest boy I ever met."

If I had to choose one moment to live within my heart / it would be that tender moment / recalling how we started /

---

* "That Sunday, That Summer," words and music by Joe Sherman and George David Weiss, 1963.

*Darling it would be when you smiled at
me that way / that Sunday, that summer /
Go on, kiss him, go on and kiss him*

I rather think we did kiss on that first date. I think I fell in love with you instantly. You treated me like a lady, you were kind and gentle and funny.

There are special moments that I live within my heart. It was always that special look when we were in a crowd, as though we had a secret that no one else knew. It was the searching for me at the community pool when you came home from a trip. I looked up, saw you, walked over to you and you took me in your arms and kissed me in front of the whole world. We had been married many years by then, but you could set my heart singing and my body yearning.

It was the thousands of moments that I was so proud to be your wife.

It was you abandoning me in Eureka, California, in a gift shop—without money, credit cards, my whole purse—because we'd miscommunicated. The sight of you walking down the street blissfully unaware as I finally caught up to you always makes me laugh.

*"Go on, kiss him, go on and kiss him /
and if I had to chose just one moment to
live within my heart / it would surely be
that moment recalling how we started /
darling, it would be when you smiled at
me / that way / that Sunday / that summer / If I had to chose just one day"*

Once again it is music that has been a catharsis for me. For months I have been feeling little joy and a deep sadness. It seems as though, as time goes on, no one remembers him anymore. I had this CD on my stereo in the car and must have heard the song hundreds of times in the last several months. Suddenly, one day I really listened to the lyrics and started weeping. I realized that those moments are what are really important, what keep him alive in my heart—the great joy we had in simply loving each other so well. ~

A Funny Thing Happened on the Way to My Exercise Bike

I have started to enjoy my exercise bike. Who would have ever thought that would happen! I've been listening to National Public Radio while I ride, and it is fun. I will not look at the clock until the song or talk is over. Today they were playing classical music. I must admit I am not a classical music fan, but I guess being exposed to something makes one appreciate it more.

Today there was a lovely piece on with a long violin solo. I closed my eyes and felt like I had an out-of-body experience. I raised my arms and played along with the artist. It was as though I was one with some ethereal presence. It was such a holy experience. I felt very close to God. When the piece ended and I looked at the clock, sixteen minutes had passed.

It is a gift. I get my exercise, calm my spirit, and some days enjoy a good laugh if Garrison Keillor is on. I learn things I never thought I would care about. It is almost like going to college.

Whereas last year putting fifteen minutes on the bike was shear torture, this year I am up to thirty minutes with no problem. It is such a handy thing to have. I could never understand how Clete could ride that sucker for an hour or more. Well, I don't think I'll ever stay on it that long. However, I can now understand why he liked it. It does make me feel better mentally and physically. Glory be. ~

Dear Matt

Dear Matt,

I've been wanting to write a letter to you for some time, but somehow have not gotten it done. After talking to you yesterday, I decided now is the time.

I hope I did not make you sadder about your Dad yesterday. It is hard for all of us. The enclosed page from one of my daily devotionals so reminded me of you when you were growing up that I knew I wanted to write to you. Both of the devotionals are nice, but the one for February 12 really made me smile and think of you.

All those nights you used to come into our bedroom and sit and talk and talk to us—they are some of my best memories. It was such a pleasure to have a child who actually seemed to like his parents' company. Dad and I both thank you for that.

Being a parent of four children can be a challenge, but also a joy. The challenge is that with four there always seemed to be somebody going through a "stage." (Sometimes that somebody was even Mom or Dad!)

It is especially rewarding to have you grow up and become a friend and not just our child. To have you marry a wonderful girl I love as a daughter and a dear friend. And of course to have the greatest grandson in the world.

I really did live a fairytale life with your Dad. Even in the worst times of our marriage I knew that when the chips were down I could count on him. We were both so zany that it made life fun. When he started his love affair with his bicycle, I learned to fill my time with quilting. When he had his first bicycle accident and was off work for ten weeks, he learned to love to read for pleasure. We shared the love of being EMTs and giving back to the community. Somewhere along the way he started going to plays with me at the Fulton. At first I think he did it just to please me, but then he learned to love the theater also.

Marriage can be like a dance and we are not always hearing the same music. Sometimes we want to run away from all the craziness of life and have time for ourselves, and that can be a good thing. Because in the end we finally realize that the person who can drive us crazy is also the only person who can make our life a magical thing.

Your Dad was always my safe place and I miss that more than words can say.

Just treasure your wife and always treat her well. Stay close to Ben and always be a good example to him, as your Dad was to you. Keep laughing and having fun.

With all my love, from your zany Mom

P.S. This letter is for Pam to read too, even though I wrote it to you. Love you, Pammy Sue. ~

Still Lost but Trying

It has been a long time since I have written anything—probably five or six months. It has been a difficult time. I guess I think I should be doing better than I am.

In the beginning, although it was terrible, there was this sense of somehow being able to learn and do all the things I had to deal with. Some days, that gave me a feeling of "well done," even as I struggled with the grief and a world turned upside down.

Now it has been over three years and I still suffer at times from a terrible depression. I miss him just as much and at times feel separated from him. Worse yet is the feeling that the world has forgotten him. The things I must deal with are no easier—different, but not easier. The financial market—done deal and out of my control. My fall was a big setback—not just the fall but the fear that if anything serious happens to me I am really alone to deal with it. What decisions will I have to make? Who will sit with me in a doctor's office and be my advocate?

Then there are the nightmares. The first was dreaming that our two bottom dresser drawers were not only empty but gone—taken out of the dresser and gone. I got up (in my dream) in a panic and started going through the other drawers to see if his clothes were there. Why, I thought, would he take both drawers and leave? I awoke in a panic, feeling as though a donkey had kicked me in the stomach. Then I realized he was dead.

Alta tells me those drawers being gone represent the fact that he is gone forever, and the bottom drawers represent the fact that the bottom fell out of my world. Explained like that, it makes perfect sense.

A day or two later I was dreaming that I had to talk to him, had to resolve something. It seemed we were in some sort of parking lot—at least there were lots of cars around. It was Clete but did not quite look like him; he was heavier and had dark hair. He seemed to be working on a car and had a grease rag in his hands. I said, "We need to talk, I want to talk to you." He said, "No, I am not going to talk to you.

"But why? Why won't you talk to me?" He kept backing up and using his hands in a gesture to keep me at arms' length. I awoke terribly upset, realized he was dead, and started to cry. At our next session, Alta had no explanation for that dream. We got onto another topic. I will have to ask her about that.

It is odd because the night before the last dream I had prayed, "Please, God, just let me see him in a dream and talk to him. After I calmed down I thought, I guess I should be careful what I pray for.

A week or so later I was rewarded, or maybe *blessed* is a better word. I had gotten awake after a fairly good night's sleep and saw him leaning over the bed to see if I was awake. He would do that sometimes when he was alive. Then he moved to the foot of the other side of the bed and sat down. He had on a suit, had his legs crossed, and looked so handsome. I was about to say, I'm awake, come on over and give me a hug. Suddenly, as quickly as he had appeared, he was gone. It was a wonderful moment.

My children have been great. The girls and I seem to have put our differences behind us. The boys, as usual, are there for me. I am tired of being sad, tired of fighting depression. I was again truly suicidal; the only thing that stops me is knowing how much that would hurt Clete and, of course, the children.

Certainly part of the problem has been the long dreary winter weather lingering into spring. The other is all the heartache and misery going on around me in the lives of friends and acquaintances. I know I must stop thinking I can fix everything. I can't, nor should I try. I can't say, "Are you people crazy? Cherish what you have, life is short, make the most of it." Did I? No, not always, and besides, it's not my life. If someone wants to screw theirs up, the most I can do is listen and try to keep my mouth shut. If listening gets too hard, then I must retreat to my solitude.

One of the pluses this past year is my volunteer work at the Lititz library, leading a story time for three- to five-year-olds. It has been a real challenge and sometimes I walk in there exhausted. I walk out exhilarated, some-times shaking my head at the antics of eleven energetic preschoolers. I love them all and try to put some fun in little people's lives that are far too structured in other areas. I hope I'm making a difference in their lives. They are surely making a difference in mine.

Doing that, still working, and taking classes down-town at Quest in addition to running my household fills my time as much as I want it filled. I also am re-sponsible for getting greeters for the church and I some-times help collate mailings. I enjoy doing mindless jobs like that.

Of course my timeouts at Starbucks, or at Borders or Higher Grounds, are lifesavers. My tickets to the theater are great—very expensive, but I have decided it is an expense that is well spent as I ask friends or Alan to join me. It has been a startling eye opener to see how much Alan enjoys the theater. Who would have thought?

I wish I could spend more girlfriend time with Jackie, but her life it so screwy that does not happen often. She has been my rock through all of this. I can tell her and Sylvia anything and they still love me.

I am hoping as the weather gets sunny and warmer I will come out of this funk. Last night Paige stopped by and I was delighted to see her. She brought me a lovely bunch of tulips for Easter. We had a good time talking and we have really bonded (and Bethany) since I started with the kids at the library. They give me tips and just laugh and laugh at my stories of frustration and amazement at how much time I put into having to prepare for a half-hour story time.

I hope that someday life, if I must live it, will be good again. I am very anxious to get up to the cemetery and put fresh flowers on the big guy's grave. What a guy he was and what a life we lived! Praise God and good for us. ~

Playing in the Sun

Saturday I went to the cemetery to put silk flowers on Clete's grave for the winter. I had been putting it off, but it was a beautiful day and I felt the urge. It was late afternoon and the sun was still high in the sky. As I finished, I turned to look at the western sky. It was very unusual. The sun was a small orb covered by grayish clouds so that it hardly shone through.

The sky looked like the ocean, filled with small whitecaps surrounding the sun, all over the western sky. The view from the cemetery is always spectacular. Little did I know what a show I was in for.

As I stood looking at the sun, suddenly I noticed a bright, narrow white light completely surrounding it. It glowed like a neon light and seemed to move in circles. Suddenly, behind the sun there were more brilliant white lights jumping side to side and up and down as though someone was having a wonderful time dancing or playing. As I watched, fascinated, I had to smile. I thought, OK, Clete, I get it. You are having a marvelous time, you are all right, and you want me to know that.

Then, in an instant the entire sky around the dancing sun turned a beautiful deep shade of pink. I stood there awestruck—it was so beautiful. It seemed to last forever. Finally I turned to go back down the hill, but I stopped and looked again. As I stared at the panorama I thought to myself, I have seen the face of Jesus. I do not mean that literally, but symbolically. At that instant, the sun and the clouds returned to normal.

For the first time since Clete's death I felt a great peace, that his soul was finally at rest. My soul was calm. It was truly a God moment. ~

"Then we sat on the edge of the Earth with our feet dangling over the side, and marveled that we had found each other."

Erik Dillard

Last Night I Had a Dream

Last night I had a dream. I remember as I went to bed I had such a strong desire to have him back again, to be able to talk to him. In my dream he had been away, probably on a hunting trip, and I was so anxious for him to come home. Whenever he was gone for some time, the homecomings were always special.

In my dream I was outside in a garden, the weather was mild, late summer or fall. I was standing by a hedge and saw him coming toward me. I joyously started walking toward him and he was on the other side of the low hedge. As I smiled and reached for him to hug me, he looked down and said something to the effect that he did not want to do that. I was very hurt and asked, "But why? What is the matter? What's wrong?" He just made a motion with his hands for me to stay back. I remember thinking, no, this time we are going to talk about it. He looked so like himself. We were maybe in our middle years.

I started to wake up and wanted so much to go back to sleep to resolve this, to learn why he was rejecting me. He looked so slim and handsome. I was devastated and did not want the dream to end. I wanted to talk things over with him. At that point I knew that he had died, but I wanted so much to be able to talk about us and our life.

It was a Sunday morning and I had to get up for church. It was with such a sense of loss that I lay in bed for a while trying to make sense of this dream and wondering why most of the few dreams I'd had about him never had a good ending. I felt devastated, as though I had lost him all over again.

As I wondered what could have possibly triggered me to have a dream like that, I remembered I had been going through some files that day and had come upon a large folder of paperwork from his accident and death. Among the papers was a police report I had not seen, or at least did not remember having seen, before. It was very descriptive of the accident. I put the file back, deciding that I really did not want to relive all that again. What was done was done.

I must ask Alta what she makes of this dream. Even at work the following Friday, my friends noticed that I was very quiet. I simply could not shake the sadness of that dream, the longing I had to have the dream continue and have a better ending. ~

I Did Not Make My Bed for Two Days

I think I can count on the fingers of one hand how many times I have not made my bed in my entire life. I was in a very down mood and just decided one day I would not make my bed. The next day I looked at the mess and thought, what the heck, I'll give myself one more day to get out of this funk. It felt good to not care a hoot.

I don't exactly know what started it. One thing is, it's the first Friday I went to work with my new glasses. I had a heck of a time on my computer, plus my left eye had been hurting. So I was pretty upset about that. Was there something wrong with my eye? With my glasses? I felt really rotten until I got home. After a few days it felt much better, so we'll see how it goes at work tomorrow.

I was doing my devotionals and for some reason I picked up Clete's Bible, which I had not touched for at least two years. I mark my Bible all over the place, but he did not. He had only two passages marked in the very beginning of his Bible. One was Colossians 3:13 and the other was Lamentations 3:22–33. I flipped to Lamentations, and there was my answer—verses 31 to 33:

> For men are not cast off
> by the Lord forever.
> Though He brings grief, He
> will show compassion,
> so great is His unfailing love.
> For He does not willingly

bring affliction
or grief to the children of men.

I felt a powerful feeling of peace wash over me.

If a plane goes down, exactly whose time was it? The pilot's? And for that reason hundreds of people died? The whole idea to me is insane. The only thing that gives me peace is that accidents happen. Why or how, we sometimes will never know, but to blame God seems to me a pretty shoddy thing to do. When they happen, I know from personal experience that He is there every step of the way with those of us who are left behind, and for that I am eternally grateful.

The whole experience pulled me pretty much out of my funk. So, I am feeling more upbeat and life looks pretty good again.

Today I made my bed. ~

Dear Alta

Dear Alta,

I have no snappy title for this letter to you.* How do I put into words all that I am feeling? I have been thinking about it and waiting for some great inspiration. So far today I got up, dressed, put on some records (yes, actual records!), took my time doing my devotions, read the paper, made some chicken salad—probably the second time in four years—and baked a chocolate cake—another rarity.

I cannot adequately express all that you have meant to me on this journey. As I look back at the beginning, I see that I was in shock far longer then I realized at the time. It seems like a miracle to have been put in touch with the perfect guide to lead me through the dark days and nights.

As we talked Monday about Clete's accident, I thought, although it was painful, I do not ever want to forget those thirty hours I had with him. I count myself blessed to have been there to "fiercely protect him," as I said in the eulogy at his memorial service.

As we talked about my ability to do things alone, it made me think. I do need alone time, but that is not to say I would not rather have him here with me in the lonely evenings, beside me in our double bed to keep me warm and safe.

---

* Written to my therapist upon her retirement.

You taught me so much. As I dealt with my issues, you always cautioned me not to "burn my bridges." That was good advice and I stop and think things through a lot more than I used to. Clete is there with me at those times also. I wonder how he would have handled some of these hurdles. Sometimes I do things as he would have and sometimes I don't.

Last Friday night, for some reason I had a painful crying jag as I yearned for him so desperately. In a way, that can be a relief, because as the years go by, sometimes he feels so far away and that makes me incredibly sad.

You and I have shed many tears over these years, but oh we have shared much laughter also. We have talked politics, religion, and silly, goofy things. You encouraged me in my writing, in my love of taking classes and reading.

I wish for you a happy new life as you deal with much change of your own. To have had a career in which you have touched so many lives must be very fulfilling for you, and at times, I am sure, very painful.

Sometimes others' words can express our feelings better than we can. I share the following with you:

> "In everyone's life, at some time, our inner fire goes out. It is then burst into flame by an encounter with another human being. We should all be thankful for those people who rekindle the inner spirit." (Albert Schweitzer)

And this one:

> "A friend is one who joyfully sings with you when you are on the mountain top

and silently walks beside you through the valley." (William Arthur Ward)

These quotes say it better than I ever could. It has been a great journey, one I will treasure always. Thank you, dear friend, and may your journey be joyful.

I close with a quote from Rose Kennedy's memoir: "It has been said that time heals all wounds. I don't agree. The wounds remain. Time—the mind protecting it's sanity—covers them with some scar tissue and the pain lessens, but it is never gone."

I agree with her, but it is people like you who put salve on our wounds and make them bearable, enable us to look at life again and decide it is good.

Bless you, Alta.

Nan ~

Two Different Kinds of Journals

For years my husband and I used daily devotionals. Because of our different schedules, we usually did them at different times. We both used *The Upper Room,* the Bible, and *Daily Guideposts.* At the end of each month in the *Guideposts* is a page on which to write your thoughts or prayers. Clete used that page more than I did because I kept a separate journal.

One day one of the *Guideposts* authors wrote about saying nightly prayers with his daughter. As they came to the name of her grandmother who had recently died, the daughter said, "We can drop Grandma; she's off the list." That absolutely cracked me up. Off the list but with God. Not a bad trade-off. That was the only journal I kept until Clete died. It was about three-quarters filled. For a while I could not function and did not pick it up for at least a week or two. When I did, I saw he had written a note to me in it, his last one, on Valentine's Day: "I love you, honey. I hope you have a good day." I had smiled as I wrote back, "I love you too, Mr. Thinker!" That referred to a private joke. He'd had only one more week to live.

As time went on and I read back over the ten months before he died, it was very painful. He'd had a long-time heart problem, but as heart problems go it was the best kind to have and was well managed. However, it was discovered that he needed a stent and they used a medicated one. It was supposed to be an in-and-out procedure, but because they had to switch his medication to one that could have life-threatening side effects, he was in for a week. Indeed, he could not tolerate the medication and had to be put on one they very seldom use anymore, and never on anyone young because of the potential side effects. Indeed, within several months it had destroyed his thyroid gland. While he was in the hospital he developed a hernia. That could not be operated on for six months because of the dangers of operating too soon after receiving the medicated stent.

He was more uncomfortable with the hernia than with anything else that went on those last months. A month or so before he was to have the hernia surgery he was diagnosed with bladder cancer. Now we were dealing with three doctors to decide the best way to go. We always gave Dr. Clark, his cardiologist, the last say on what was done when. It was decided to do the hernia surgery at six months, wait three weeks, and then do the cancer surgery.

The prognosis after the surgery was not good. Although my first reaction was "Oh, that's good," Dr. Del Terzo said, "No, it is not." I replied that I knew that, but to me the worst diagnosis would have been to remove his bladder. They removed several masses, but the cancer had not penetrated into his kidney. The doctor's advice was to take a month off (for which I am eternally grateful) and come back, but because of the terrible side effects he would advise no treatment and would just scope him (Clete hated that procedure) every three months to make sure it had not recurred. We did get a second opinion from an oncologist, and he concurred.

In addition, I was dealing with my older sister, who badly needed to give up her home and move into an assisted-living facility. Finally, with much reluctance, she made that decision. I then spent the last summer of my husband's life helping my niece clean out my sister's house (she was a hoarder) and get it ready for sale.

When I read back over those ten months, it was a real shocker to me. I forgot how frightened I was. I simply thought I had handled many difficult situations OK. Of course I knew we'd been short with each other. He handled things very calmly, unless there was a crisis, when he would become very frightened and need me very much. I could calm him down and then he was OK. The flip side of that was that sometimes he felt smothered. Through it all he kept on working and riding bike. I was OK with that unless he was taking unnecessary risks too soon.

In my journal I continually mention how frightened I was. I prayed for strength and patience, and sometimes I simply could not pray at all.

That was one prayer journal I did not throw away when it was full after he died. Occasionally through the years I would reread it. It always upset me and made me feel that I should have done better. Finally I read it again, just a few weeks ago, and decided the time had come to destroy it. That part of our life I did not want to relive anymore. We both did the best we could, and useless regrets and what ifs would not change anything.

It was a huge step forward. ~

"When I was 5 years old, my mother always told me that happiness was the key to life. When I went to school, they asked me what I wanted to be when I grew up. I wrote down "happy." They told me I didn't understand the assignment. I told them they didn't understand life." John Lennon

Mother Teresa spent her life serving others. Her words are not those of someone who was a slave to her work but offer a philosophy of living:

"People are often unreasonable and self-centered. Forgive them anyway.

"If you are kind, people may accuse you of ulterior motives. Be kind anyway.

"If you are honest, people may cheat you. Be honest anyway.

"If you find happiness, people may be jealous. Be happy anyway.

"The good you do today may be forgotten tomorrow. Do good anyway.

"Give the world the best you have and it may never be enough. Give your best anyway.

"For you see, in the end, it is between you and God. It was never between you and them anyway."

The trick to living a full life is to marry John Lennon's words with Mother Teresa's actions.

Intelligencer Journal, June 1, 2011

Breathing Air

"The church has not always been good at acknowledging how much life hurts," said Alison Bair, whose youngest daughter died of brain cancer at the age of eight. In an article about the Blue Christmas service held a month before Christmas at First Presbyterian Church in Lancaster, Alison, associate in worship ministries, described herself as "under water" after her child's death, even though she was functioning very well and people admired her for her strength. "It took me four years before I was beginning to breathe air again," she said.

That piece was one of the greatest helps for me in my long journey. As the months and then the years progressed, I felt very much as though I was "under water." I would take comfort from remembering her words. As I reached and passed the fourth year, I was still very much "under water" much of the time. I wondered if this was how it would always be for me.

There was also much turmoil in the church I belong to, and at the same time the atmosphere at the job I had held for twenty-four years was getting really bad and I knew it would get no better. Quitting the job would mean rethinking my finances—all this as Christmas approached. I always find Christmas very difficult.

One thing I have learned these past four and a half years is to think things through and not act in haste. I took several weeks to decide what to do. I decided to reach out to our pastor, who had been let go, and to stay in the church but back off from my involvement. As for the job, I had been thinking for some time that another year was all I would do. After some hard thought I decided to quit in three months. Things were definitely not going to change; a job I had loved had become a job that was no longer fun. I gave notice at work and felt a great peace about that.

Losing Alta as my therapist was also a great loss.

Then suddenly I felt a change I can't describe. I no longer dreaded Christmas as I had the first four Christmases after Clete's death. I really did feel as though I was "breathing air" again. It was a miracle.

Do I still get down? Of course, but it is not the terrible hopeless feeling all the time. I seem to be able to communicate with my daughters better.

I do hope to find a volunteer job for Fridays—one that will be rewarding. I don't want to spend any more time at a job I once loved and no longer enjoy. What will I do with the rest of my life? Well, at seventy-seven I think I have earned the right to do pretty much what I want. Go to college, write a book (always a good thing to say because I'd never get it done, but a wonderful answer to those people who say, but what do you DO?). Then there is parachuting out of an airplane, spending time at the beach, hanging out at coffee shops, reading to my heart's content.

I have worked too hard to get to where I am today. I will miss Clete for the rest of my life. I certainly have no desire to live to an old, old age. But what is, is, and I want just to find contentment and sometimes even joy.

I know that I am a very lucky lady. I have had a great life and have many marvelous memories of our life together. ~

A Grateful Heart

My love,

As I pass the five-year mark of your death, how do I begin to tell you how grateful I am for the life we had together? I do not know if we are unique in the fact that our love grew and matured as we grew, and grew older. When I think of all our years together, I am amazed at all we lived through—the happy times, the stormy times, the just plain everyday times, and the mountaintop times.

You were always my rock, my safe place. I knew that even when things were hard and sometimes so busy that we barely had time to catch our breath.

You were fun. You put up with my moods and my crazy antics. I think I brought a sense of silliness to your life. We had the same zany sense of humor.

We both had a deep sense of what is right and wrong—a passion for treating people with respect and fairness—at least most of the time. We became very interested in politics and I miss talking to you about current events, a lot—although I think you would be going crazy, as am I, over the lack of respect in today's world.

I miss sharing our bed, our pillow talk, our love life, waking up to see you beside me on the weekends, hearing about each other's day.

We raised four children and I think we did a pretty good job. They all married well and I think they are happy. I am so sorry you did not live to see Ben grow up. He is a fine young man and you would be proud of him. He is a Gibble through and through—tall and lean, but with the Smith facial features.

I feel so blessed that I am not a bitter woman because of your being taken from me so cruelly. I feel blessed because we had each other so many years, even if it was not nearly as many as I wanted. I miss you terribly and yearn for us to be together again.

While it is often said we do not appreciate what we have until we lose it, I do not find that to be true. Certainly we were not always what we wanted each other to be, but I always knew that I was a very lucky woman. I trusted you and always valued the kind of man you were—good, kind, humble. I laugh when I think about how, when you were exasperated, you would throw up your hands and say, "Mein Gott"—the Pennsylvania Dutch in you. It was neat that we enjoyed the simple things: evenings on the deck, talking about the day, watching TV or reading a book together, taking walks and bike rides. I could outwalk you and you sure could outride me. Now I can no longer take long walks as I once did, but I can still go for short rides on my bike, and I really enjoy it—most days. You loved sports; me, not so much, unless one of the children was involved. I love the theater and you learned to enjoy that too, to my great delight.

One of the things we most enjoyed was going to the Horse Inn or Hall's Cafe on a Saturday night. It was always relaxing when we went there; we always connected and really talked things over on those nights. I miss that a lot. We both always got the same thing. I always had a glass of wine. You did not.

I loved the way you cared about clothing. You dressed well and I was always proud to be seen with you. You loved me to look nice, and to this day I still dress to please you, my love.

We took wonderful vacations—twice to Europe, to Prince Edward Island, to our wonderful Cape May, a

long trip west in the car—and my personal favorite was when we flew to San Francisco and drove the Pacific

Coast Highway to the north. I loved that trip. We flew to the Grand Canyon and then west to San Diego. Then there was our beloved Rutledge Inn and Cottages in Vermont, where we went with the children for many years. Didn't we almost have it all?

On Sunday there was an article in the paper about the man who was the guardian angel of Route 66. They wrote about Seligman, Arizona, and I laughed. We bought a mug there that has Route 66, Lilo's Café on it. Remember on that trip that we wanted to drive the old Route 66 and ended up going down the most treacherous road I was ever on to get to this ghost town where Clark Gable and one of his wives spent their honeymoon. It was one of the few times I was really frightened; I think my eyes were closed most of the way and I was squealing OHHHHHHHH. We didn't pass a vehicle the whole way down, but when we got there, the town was full of people. We asked, how did you get here? Oh, they said, there is another easy road to get here! When we left, I suggested we take the other road back. True to the Gibble mentality, you said, oh no, it will be OK to go back the same way. I thought you were insane, but actually it was not as bad going in the other direction. Maybe it was because I was on the mountain side on the way back instead of on the from-here-to-eternity side, where one false move would send us off the mountain. Adventures—we sure had them on our trips.

So, my darling, thanks for the memories, for the love we shared, for the life we led. I could not have asked for better.

Your faithful wife,
Nan ~

Another Dream

In the summer of 2011, Manheim had torrential rains. My family room got flooded. It was an expensive clean-up, but not a tragedy. Many people in Manheim lost their homes and all their belongings.

I did have a terrible dream right after the flood happened.

I was being swept downstream, fighting for my life, with no one to rescue me, when suddenly I was carried into a beautiful green meadow. I was naked, with some kind of green blanket covering me. The surrounding countryside looked calm and peaceful; people were sitting around drinking lemonade, smiling and laughing. I called out for someone to help me, to warm me, because I was terribly cold. No one seemed to see me. I felt utterly abandoned.

Unlike most of my dreams, I remembered this one vividly. It was symbolic of the last five and a half years of my life. Alone and abandoned, without the anchor who had kept me safe. ~

I Miss His Voice

I saw a movie this week. One of the lines made me weep: "I miss his voice. I miss his voice telling me he loves me." That one sentence summed up exactly the pain I feel, the yearning just to hear his voice.

Just to be able to have a conversation with him. To speak in the husband-and-wife shorthand in which you can finish each other's sentences. To hear him watching TV and having his conversation with himself as he cheers on his team or groans at a dumb play. To tell me about his day, his ride, the kids on the van, his coworkers. To see his face and hear his pleasure: "You made apple dumplings!"

We were so lucky that we loved each other so well and so long. What a grand adventure we had. I have so many happy memories: living in four different places in a two-month span in Chicago; New Rochelle and only one apartment, but two different jobs in just over a year; driving the Boston Post Road to my first job, and to the ferry depot to take the ferry across to the island for my second. Sometimes he was on weekend duty or out of town for his job—and then, when he came home, I would hear his voice.

I so wish I had his voice on our answering machine. He did not like when his voice was on because he thought it sounded terrible. We all think our voice is terrible on an answering machine.

One time we were at a restaurant and having a great time catching up on all we had to tell each other. We were laughing and of course 1 was, as usual, talking with my hands. One of the wait staff told us as we left that it was so wonderful to see a couple eating together and actually talking to each other and enjoying each other's company. We each heard the other's voice and, in our pleasure, gave pleasure to others also.

There is a certain magic in those memories.

1 miss his voice—1 miss his voice telling me he loves me. ~

A Simpler Time

The following two pieces were written many years ago as letters to our children. At some point in my life I realized that children seem to think of parents as just parents and nothing more. They neither know nor care, until it is much too late, exactly who their parents were.

What shaped their lives? I grew up with many aunts and both grandparents on my mother's side of the family. Before the days of television, front-porch sitting was an evening institution and the neighbors visited back and forth. If you were very quiet you could hear some juicy family gossip. If my mother and my aunts noticed I was listening, they immediately started speaking Pennsylvania Dutch.

We had the run of the neighborhood. Everyone knew everyone else, and woe to the child who got out of line.

It was a simpler time. I can still smell and feel the autumn days with their crackling leaf piles to jump in and the horse chestnuts from which we made pipes.

I have no idea what years I wrote these pieces, because I did not date them.

I am glad I found them as I was going through my files. Will they give my children pleasure? I do not know. But they certainly gave me a great deal of excitement and joy when I found them. ~

Chicago

If any of my children had gotten married as young as I did, I would have thrown ten fits. I was out of high school a little more than a year and eighteen years of age. I had no money. In fact, I cashed in my Christmas Club to get fifty dollars to buy my wedding outfit.

From the day of our first date until the day I said "I do," I had known my husband-to-be for only nine months. We chose the fourth of July to get married because Clete had a three-day pass from the Army and the fourth fell on a Friday, giving us a three-day weekend to have our honeymoon.

Our honeymoon consisted of driving down the Skyline Drive in Virginia and winding our way to Camp Blackstone for a week. I stayed in a barracks with the other wives. Clete was on duty during the day and joined me at night. We slept on army cots and at night you could hear all the couples pushing the cots together to make a double to sleep in—or whatever else they had in mind.

After the honeymoon, I returned to Manheim, to my job as a secretary, until August, when Clete finished basic training and was posted on assignment. He was in the medical corp because at the time he belonged to a pacifist church. He was assigned the job of food inspector for the army. At that time the food inspectors were assigned to the office of the veterinarian. Go figure.

To learn to be a food inspector, he first had to attend a school in Chicago for two months. I was thrilled.

I was going to the big city. Me. *Me.* Little old me from the sticks was going to be a big-city girl.

Clete would rather have had me wait at home while he went out and found us a place to live, but I insisted that I wanted to go right away and that it would all work out. Love prevailed and off we went. My mother later said that as we drove off in our 1949 red Plymouth convertible loaded to the gills, the box in the rear window boldly proclaimed in large letters KOTEX.

We drove straight through, stopping occasionally for short naps. At that time, in the early 1950s, the trip took about fifteen hours. We got there and could find no room at the inn. No one seemed to want to rent an apartment to two hayseeds from Pennsylvania. Clete wanted to send me home, but I was adamant about staying. My pride would not let me go home and admit I had given up. So, we spent our first night in Chicago in a motel, leaving everything packed in the car.

The next day we contacted the brother of some friends from home who were involved with Bethany Biblical Seminary, the college for students learning to be ministers of the Church of the Brethren—the church to which my husband belonged. Since it was summer and most of the students were off on summer break, we were able to stay in a student apartment. We moved into place number two in Chicago in the space of two days. It was great. The only problem was that the couple who usually occupied that particular apartment came back early for the fall semester, so after several weeks we had to move to another apartment in the same complex. That was place number three in Chicago.

September came as September does and all the students returned for classes. This of course necessitated another move. This time we found a very unusual apartment. It was a kind of community apartment. Everyone had their own bedroom, but we shared a common bathroom, living room, and kitchen. That was place number four in Chicago. Someone once asked me if we were rent hopping. Keep in mind that we were only in Chicago for two months. During that time we lived in four different places. Only young lovers could handle that.

The last place was by far the most memorable. Chicago was where I first doubted God's wisdom in putting all creatures on the Earth. This was because every time I wanted to take a bath I had to yell for Clete to come kill the cockroaches. It was so dirty in Chicago that on one memorable occasion I ironed one of Clete's white dress shirts about five times because every time I ironed it a sleeve dragged on the floor and I had to rewash it. Those were the days when you sprinkled your clothes to iron them and used starch on the collars and cuffs. It might take some historical research on the part of my children to understand that concept.

We ate a lot of Campbell's soup in Chicago, and toasted cheese sandwiches. That was all I knew how to make. Fortunately, my sister Jean had given me a *Better Homes and Gardens* cookbook for a wedding present and I learned to cook out of that. I never did cook like a Pennsylvania Dutch woman.

Still, I loved Chicago. I loved going to open-air concerts on the edge of the lake. I loved the downtown. We lived in the middle of Chicago. I worked for Sears Roebuck in their typing pool and that was downtown also. I don't remember how I got to work. I had no car because Clete needed it to go to school. Perhaps I walked or rode the bus. In any case, I felt very "big cityish." I loved the "El," the above-ground trains that took you from one place to another in Chicago. I felt very glamorous and grown up—this little girl from Pennsylvania.

It was a wonderful time and I wouldn't trade any of it. Not the crazy moving around, or the roach-infested apartment, or the concerts on the lake, or the bright lights of the big city, or being with the person I loved most in all the world.

Chicago—it really was a wonderful town. ~

New York, New York

When I was very young, I thought the most glamorous thing in the world would be to be a private secretary to some big-shot executive. I would be very efficient and indispensable. I'd wear a neat little navy blue suit with white cuffs and a white blouse with a Peter Pan collar, small pearl earrings, and navy blue pumps.

Obviously I spent a lot of time going to the movies in the late forties.

Well, I was a private secretary for a very short period of my life. Then love intervened, and I married, followed my husband to the various army bases he was assigned to, and ended up in a typing pool. Still, to a little small-town girl like me, living in Chicago and then close to New York City did seem very glamorous.

I heard my first outdoor concert on the shores of Lake Superior, and saw my first Broadway play in New York. In New York I went to work every day on a ferryboat because I worked on Fort Slocum, an island in the middle of Long Island Sound, where my husband was based.

We lived in a third-floor attic apartment. It was hot in summer and freezing in winter. The bathroom was small with a sloped ceiling. You could sit on the toilet and, with just a slight shift of your body, brush your teeth at the same time. When you were done with your bath, you could not stand upright in the tub to dry off without hitting your head on the ceiling.

In the summer it was so hot I took to walking around the apartment in just a pair of panties—particularly when I was cooking. There was no need to worry about anyone seeing me; our windows were tiny, and besides, there was an enormous weeping willow tree right outside that obscured the view for anyone looking in.

Our landlords were an elderly couple, or at least they seemed so to me at the age of eighteen. There was one ironclad rule: no drinking allowed.

One night we were at a party thrown by the base on a ferryboat. My husband, who never drank, proceeded to get drunk as a skunk. I was not amused, particularly when he threw his arms around me and knocked my earring clean into Long Island Sound. The problem then became how to sneak him into our third-floor apartment without our landlords suspecting anything. Two army pals helped him up the two flights of narrow stairs. I told them just to dump him on the sofa as I certainly didn't want him in our bed.

The landlords somehow let me know they were well aware of the condition my husband was in when he came home; could it have been his loud singing as he was going up the stairs? They graciously overlooked the incident since we were so obviously innocents. They knew it would never happen again.

I loved the army base. Working on an island was quite an experience. I loved walking around the perimeter, except for passing the two large dogs that belonged to the camp veterinarian. They seemed to stalk me as I walked, particularly at night, when I had to walk back to the ferryboat by myself for the trip home if Clete was on night duty.

I grew. I learned to know different people from different backgrounds and religions and different regions of the country. I, who had never owned a car or driven by myself, could now maneuver through crowded city streets. I became an expert at parking in tiny parking spaces. Once, in early November, we had a snowstorm and I had to drive home all by myself, first stopping at the neighborhood market for food to eat once I got there. It was exhilarating and exciting for a young girl who previously had never been farther from home than Atlantic City, New Jersey.

My best friends were Kitty, a girl I worked with who was from New Rochelle, and the wife of an army buddy of my husband's who was from Georgia. I met some strange people too. There was the girl who had been married for nearly a year and still had not consummated her marriage. She was wondering why she didn't get pregnant. I assume she eventually figured out what the problem was since she did have a baby girl sometime later.

Everyone thought I was either Italian or Jewish because I was very dark complexioned and had dark hair and dark eyes. When they found out that wasn't true and that I was from Pennsylvania, they thought I had come from the coal regions because that was all they knew about Pennsylvania. That was when I learned it is best not to have pre-conceived notions about people and places.

I loved to go into New York City and see the sights. I felt like a big city girl. Still, we were homesick and came home to Pennsylvania every chance we got. Sunday nights we would drive back to New York and listen to all the radio programs on the car radio as we drove; *Inner-Sanctum* was particularly scary late on a rainy Sunday night. I can close my eyes and still get the same lonely feeling I would get then as we drove back to the base.

I would not trade those years for anything. Sometimes I feel like I'd do anything to have them back again—the years when we were young and anything was possible. ~

The Accident and Coffee Shops

About a month ago, as I was coming home from a bike ride, I stopped at a stop sign, looked both ways, and saw nothing on my right. On the left were a large white van and another vehicle. As they passed, I started across. I was almost across the road when I saw a red and white streak go past me. Before I knew what was happening I was airborne and my bike went out from under me. Thank God I no longer clip my feet in the pedals. I felt like I was on a magic carpet flying toward the sky. I had my eyes wide open and felt absolutely no fear. I just looked at the sky and thought, "Clete, I think I'm going to see you sooner than I thought I was." Just that quickly I fell onto the macadam, flat on my back. My head bounced several times, breaking my helmet in three places. Instantly there were four women surrounding me. One was calling 911, one asked if I wanted a towel under my neck, and one kept holding my hand and talking to me.

The ambulance arrived. I asked one of the ladies to get my medical information out of my bike bag. I remember being in the ambulance and a police officer in the ambulance smiling at me. From that point on I remember nothing until they had me in the emergency room and were transferring me to a bed.

I was sent for scans of my brain, pelvis, the whole nine yards. I felt absolutely no pain. They brought me back to the ER to await the results of the tests. I was hooked up to all kinds of stuff and just uncomfortable. The doctor came in and said when he heard the call he thought it was going to be really ugly. I replied, "I'll bet you did." He told me all the test results were negative and asked if I wanted pain pills. I said no because I wasn't hurting more than I usually do. He told me I was going to feel a lot worse the next day and again asked if I wanted some pain pills. I said no. When he asked me how I felt I said, "Well——." He asked, "Kind of like you were hit by a car?"

The doctor told me I could go home but, if I started to feel bad, to come back to the ER or go to my family doctor. In any case I was to see my family doctor in four or five days.

So there I was in my crummy cycling clothes without my cell phone and able to remember only two numbers to call for a ride home. There was no answer at either number. I hiked out to the lobby to call a cab.

After I got home I remembered I had not eaten breakfast. I decided to shower and go down to Starbucks. I walked in and the baristas said, "Nan, how are you doing?" I told them I had been hit by a car and needed some tender loving care.

They were as they always are—kind and caring—and I got a hug. For the last several years the Lititz Starbucks has been my hangout place. The staff is great and I've made friends with some of the other customers. It definitely is a *Cheers* type of place, where everybody knows your name.

When I told the staff I was writing a book, they asked what it was about. I told them and said they would be in it but, to protect the innocent, I would not use their names. "No, no," they said, I must use their names. When I asked why, Lynn said, "Because I want to be able to tell my children: see, there's my name in that book."

So, here's to Lynn, who can change his looks depending on how often he shaves; to Kristin, the boss, who keeps them all under control and has a deep and hearty laugh; to Zach, the quiet one who just left—I'll miss him; and to Chicago David, who is in culture shock getting adjusted to Lancaster County. He keeps complaining about our "mountains." I told him, we have hills, we do not have mountains. He strongly disagrees. Then there is weatherman David. He was a television weather fore-caster down in Florida. He's a character whom I try to keep under control. I fail. Andy is more low key, and he blushes. Jocelyn is one of the other bosses. She is sweet and quieter. There is little Candice; I think the guys pick on her a bit. They will deny it. Theresa just started. I'll remember her name; she was named after St. Therese, the "little flower." Val is very efficient, kind, and patient. Robbie got hit by a car while riding his bike home from work; he was hurt worse than I was but is going to be OK. Santina is brand new, and Ashley is petite and holds her own against the guys. Shawna moved here from Cali-fornia. One day, when she was on break, I asked her what brought her to Pennsylvania. Without missing a beat she said, "God." I burst out laughing and asked, how so? I then heard her story. I cannot forget Tiffany; she is usually very quiet and serious, but one day I heard her laugh and laugh. It was delightful.

That is what is so wonderful about places like Star-bucks: everyone has a story, everyone is unique and special.

So, to the Starbucks gang, and to the people in the other coffee shops I have hung out in over the years (especially Ashley and Kathy, the owners of Higher Grounds Cafe in Mt. Joy), I thank you from the bottom of my heart for your kindness and craziness, your com-passion and love. ~

The Doctor Visit

I went down to see Dr. Russo the week after the accident. He already knew about it, but before we got to the
accident, we talked about another concern I had.

I told him I simply will not give up riding. It is the one
place I feel really close to Clete, and I can understand why
he loved it so much. The risks for him were much greater
than the risks for me, but all of life is a risk of some kind
or another. It is good for my knees, not so good for my
hands, but everything is some kind of trade-off.

He asked how my family felt about it. I told him they
were not happy campers, but that was their problem. In
raising four children there were many times that I was
not always a happy camper. I am far beyond the age
where I have to ask my children for permission. Having
said that, I asked him what my doctor thinks about this.

Dr. Russo said, "I understand what you are saying,
that this brings you great peace and closer to Clete and
I am not going to tell you not to do it." That is why I
love and respect my family doctor. However, as he was
leaving the room he turned and said, "Although I must
say, you sure took several years off *my* life!" I was still
laughing as he walked out the door. Dr. Russo had never
met Clete, but he knows the story. He has walked with me
on this journey and I appreciate him and his entire staff. ~

New Horizons

Psalm 51:8 — "Let me hear the sound of joy and glad-ness; and though you have crushed me and broken me, I will be happy once again."

I had to think a bit about what to call this final piece in my odyssey. I've been surprised at how many ups and downs I've had in even the last six months or so.

One day it suddenly occurred to me that I was ready to move on, literally and figuratively. I no longer needed to live in this home we shared for the last nine years of Clete's life. I realized that wherever I live, it is no longer the house that matters. What matters is that he lives in my heart, no matter where my physical home is.

The effort and expense of the upkeep of the house began to wear on me, as well as the physical task of taking care of a three-story home. I was simply tired. It just seemed overwhelming. Besides, it is very lonely living alone. I need to be around people and have some sense of community.

I put my name in for an apartment in a lovely retirement community less then a mile from where I live. It was a very big decision for me.

As a friend and I toured the place and looked at some of the apartments they have to offer, I fell in love with it. Of course everything is a trade-off. The apartment I would love to have is simply too expensive. After the disappoint of realizing that, I came to terms with the fact that I could be happy with my second choice, although because the space will be one room smaller it will be a challenge.

It is important to do your homework. My son-in-law was a great help in doing the math for me, in helping me look at several options for how to sell all the things I will not be able to take along. I have never been a hoarder, thank heavens. A house is just a house and stuff is just stuff. I need to realize what is important to me. Having a place to continue my writing is very important.

One of the pluses of the retirement community is it feels like a European village. There is much open space inside where you can find the sun, if it is not in your apartment all day. There is also plenty of outdoor space in which to ride bike and walk.

Another plus is that I know so many people who live there, and everyone I met was so kind and friendly. Although people there respect one another's privacy, it also feels like they look out for each other.

The biggest challenge will be living in so small a space. But then I laugh and think, my goodness, we started out in one room, and then a small apartment, and then a communal apartment, all in the space of two months in Chicago. In New York we lived in a garret apartment on the third floor. Well, I hope to be on the third floor in this apartment. However, I will have a lovely balcony with a great view, *and* an elevator to get there instead of hiking up two flights of stairs. There will be two libraries, a gift shop, two cafes, a pool, a hot tub, and exercise equipment.

Those are just the physical things. What I most hope to find is peace. I want this to be my safe place. I like the analogy of an animal who, when it feels threatened, runs to its "bolt hole." For me, my home has definitely been a "bolt hole," along with visits to the cemetery and to coffee shops.

A day or two after I made the decision, a real panic attack hit as I looked too far ahead and wondered how I would do all this. I know I have the tenacity, but I get tired of being "strong." I just want to sit and weep, and have somebody hold my hand and say, "Now, now, everything will be OK. We'll all help you."

I know I am one very lucky woman. Clete and I raised four children, all of whom are in good marriages, have good jobs, and are very self-sufficient, and thanks to number four child, we have a wonderful grandson.

I was married to someone who was the light of my life. To lose him to a traumatic death was truly terrible. And yet, I am so thankful that I was with him through that last journey.

I have grown in my faith. I know sometimes I have to sit down, center myself, and be still as I let God speak to me; to sit quietly and just listen to whatever comes into my mind. It is a powerful gift that took me a long time to learn.

I think I will always struggle a bit. And I will always miss him.

I often wish for just one more chance to tell him how much I love him. Silly me, because of course he knows. Lucky me, to have led the life we lived, both the good and the bad.

Cherish the moment, for it may never come again. Nothing can take away your memories, and therefore love lives on forever. ~

Acknowledgments

Thank you to:

Alice Morrow Rowan, my editor, who encouraged me to share my journals written after Clete's death. When I would go into panic mode and feel over-whelmed, she gave me the courage to go on.

Steve Hershberger for his marketing skills and his sense of humor and compassion.

Jackie Gainer and Linda Skelly for taking time to read and critique the manuscript. Jackie has walked this journey with me.

Larry Gainer for his skill in restoring many old pho-tographs and for the cover design.

Susan Shaw for allowing me to use her photograph on the cover. It is exactly right for the book!

Jo Stauffer, my sister-in-law, and Chaplain Hayden McLean for being with me at the hospital from the very beginning and staying with me many hours as I tried to reach family members.

My children—Alan, Bethany, Paige, and Matthew—who gave me support at the hospital and cared for me so well in the weeks following Clete's death.

Dr. Peter Stewart and the staff of the emergency room and neurotrauma unit of Lancaster General Hospital.

Dr. Neil Clark, Clete's primary cardiologist. His call to my home to offer his condolences meant more to me than he will ever know.

Dr. Douglas Gohn, who arranged for me to sit down with Dr. Stewart and go over all his charts and CAT scans.

Dr. Michael Del Terzo, Clete's urologist, who gave us the gift of time off after Clete's bladder cancer surgery.

The Lititz Borough Police Department and Warwick Ambulance Association.

Alta Landis, my therapist, who with great skill and compassion helped me through all the ups and downs of a life without Clete.